Castles of England and Wales

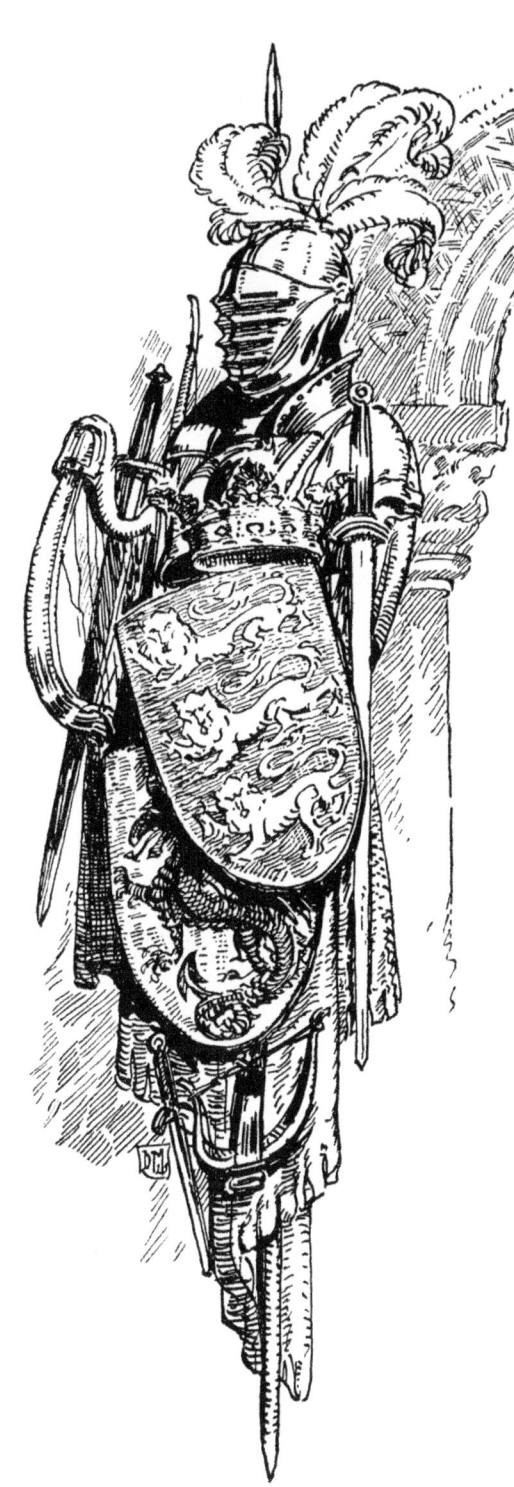

Castles of England and Wales

Described by
E. J. MACDONALD

With Illustrations by
HERBERT J. FINN

COACHWHIP PUBLICATIONS
GREENVILLE, OHIO

Castles of England and Wales, by E. J. MacDonald
Illustrated by Herbert J. Finn
© 2026 Coachwhip Publications edition

First published 1925
Edward Jackson MacDonald, no dates known
Herbert John Finn, 1860-1942
CoachwhipBooks.com

ISBN 1-61646-628-6
ISBN-13 978-1-61646-628-2

LIST OF ILLUSTRATIONS

In Colours

WINDSOR CASTLE		*Frontispiece*
ALNWICK CASTLE	*facing page*	7
ARUNDEL CASTLE	,, ,,	15
BAMBURGH CASTLE	,, ,,	23
CARISBROOKE CASTLE	,, ,,	37
CASTLE RISING	,, ,,	47
DOVER CASTLE	,, ,,	53
CHEPSTOW CASTLE	,, ,,	63
DURHAM CASTLE	,, ,,	83
RICHMOND CASTLE	,, ,,	95
BARNARD CASTLE	,, ,,	101
THE TOWER OF LONDON	,, ,,	103
WARWICK CASTLE	,, ,,	109
CARNARVON CASTLE	,, ,,	115
HARLECH CASTLE	,, ,,	119
CONWAY CASTLE	,, ,,	121

LIST OF ILLUSTRATIONS

In Black and White

	PAGE
WINDSOR CASTLE	6
ALNWICK CASTLE	13
ARUNDEL CASTLE	21
BAMBURGH CASTLE	30
CAERPHILLY CASTLE	33
PORCHESTER CASTLE	38
CORFE CASTLE	44
CASTLE RISING	51
HASTINGS CASTLE	54
DEAL CASTLE	56
WALMER CASTLE	59
WINCHELSEA CASTLE	61
CHILLINGHAM CASTLE	70
,, ,,	73
CHIRK CASTLE	77
KENILWORTH CASTLE	94
BARNARD CASTLE	101
THE TOWER OF LONDON	108
TINTAGEL CASTLE	124
THE CASTLE, NEWCASTLE	129

WINDSOR

AS it appears from the railway train, Windsor's round tower rising above the trees behind Slough becomes too familiar for comment. Straining our eyes, perhaps, to see if the standard hangs above it as a sign that the royal family is in residence, we think vaguely of the castle as a palace; a place like Hampton Court, that should be worth visiting some day. We are not like the French, who have to regard Belfort, or Toul, or Verdun, as forts commanding a pass, a river, or a road. For nearly five centuries England has been an unfortified country, and, theoretically at least, the Government would surrender at once to an enemy who succeeded in crushing the naval defence. So we have no reason to think of Windsor as "commanding" the railway; and if we approach London from the west, crossing the river at Staines, there is no thought in our minds of the garrison at Windsor giving us protection.

But anyone who undertakes the tedious journey to London by river receives another impression. By the time Oxford, Wallingford, and Reading have been passed, the Thames has become no longer the scene for a day's leisurely outing, but a highway, with Windsor towering above the river, the key to London at the end of the road.

William the Conqueror, the first ruler since the Romans to subordinate the whole of England to a unified strategic plan, was faced with the problem of safeguarding the two great approaches to London from the west—the one, that system of Roman roads that ends in Oxford Street, and the other the

Thames. In his blockade of London, William himself went as far north as Wallingford before crossing the river. Subsequently, as the defender of London, he could find neither at the Goring Gap nor at Staines a position within easy reach of London which offered a natural defence in command of both road and river. But Windsor had these advantages: its site commanded the Thames, and was within two hours' march of Staines and Maidenhead, and a long day's march of his capital. There was a bluff overlooking a bend in the river and surmounted by a mound, which had possibly been already fortified by the Romans and under the Heptarchy. And at Old Windsor, not far away, was the royal " vill " of the Saxon kings.

By the time of Edward the Confessor the military value of the riverside manor was so little appreciated that he had granted it " to Christ and the Abbey of St. Peter at Westminster." William at once resumed possession, giving the monks in exchange various manors, including " St. Patrick's Isle," which we know as Battersea. Nominally, perhaps, he intended it as a hunting-lodge, but, in fact, he threw up earthworks there which made the place as strong as any of the period.

The present shape of Windsor is an oblong enclosure forming three wards, of which the mound in the middle crowned by the keep and a ditch with a small enclosure around it makes the centre ward. Some have said that the Conqueror merely palisaded the mound and the eastern ward after the usual pattern of a Norman mound-and-bailey castle. More probably he gave it at once its present form; in fact, both Nottingham and Arundel are examples that the early Norman builders did not always limit themselves to one ward. At first, however, there were probably no stone defences, but ditch, earthen rampart, and a continuous stockade made these for a time unnecessary. In the eastern, or upper ward, were the royal lodgings.

WINDSOR

For a time the Norman kings continued to use the Confessor's "vill" at Old Windsor as a royal residence. There is no mention in the chronicles of New Windsor until Henry of Huntingdon tells us that Henry I in 1110 held his court in that place "which he himself had built," and in 1121 he married in the castle chapel his second Queen, Adela of Louvain. In other words, Henry probably did something to make Windsor particularly his own. He began, most likely, to replace the wooden defences with stone, although it is curious that the rebel Robert de Mowbray should have been imprisoned there by Rufus after the siege of Bamburgh, if there were no permanent buildings already erected.

Under Henry II a casual reference here and there in the chronicles is replaced by definite entries in the royal accounts. He was a great builder at Windsor, for he raised the Great Tower in stone, constructed four towers on the eastern curtain, and four on the south side which he connected with curtain walls; and, in addition to this, he rebuilt the royal lodgings in the upper ward, which he enclosed with a wall. Henry III brought the work of fortification to its highest point, but he also erected more magnificent buildings within the wards, so that if to-day we find Windsor a palace, we feel that it has become so without violation of its early military traditions. Matthew of Westminster, describing how Prince Edward, son of Henry III, filled Windsor with troops, spoke of the fortress-palace appropriately as "that very flourishing castle than which, at that time, there was not another more splendid within the bounds of Europe."

The only serious siege suffered by Windsor was at the hands of the Count de Nevers and the Barons in opposition to John after the signing of the Charter. For three months a large and well-equipped army assaulted the castle, but *petraria* and battering ram were used in vain until the attempt had to be abandoned. But if its strength was never seriously tried, this was merely a sign of its high reputation. By the situation which it commanded, Windsor exerted a predominant, though passive, influence upon all mediæval campaigns centring around London, and it is significant that Edward I, the greatest of English castle builders, made no improvement in its fortifications.

Edward III, who was born at Windsor, often stayed there, and added much to its tradition as a palace. Influenced by the chivalry of his age, he conceived the idea of gathering a body of knights to his Round Table " in the same manner and condition as the Lord Arthur, formerly King of England, appointed it . . . and he would cherish it according to his power." For this purpose he proceeded to build a tower in the upper ward to house a great table, and at one time he was spending £100 a week on the work. It was never finished, however, and to-day not a trace remains, for by 1348 Edward's ideas had undergone a change. He founded instead the Order of the Garter, an order of which the insignia, a garter, and the motto, *Honi soit qui mal y pense*, inevitably produced a crop of legends.

It was the foundation of the Garter Order which made Edward remodel Henry III's chapel of St. Edward as a chapel for his knights. This chapel has had a curious history. When Edward IV built the larger and more glorious St. George's Chapel at its western end, it became a Lady Chapel which Henry VII re-edified, proposing to use it as a shrine for Henry VI and a burial-place for English kings. Instead, he raised the beautiful building bearing his name at Westminster, and in course of time Cardinal Wolsey, once canon of Windsor, was to be found supervising the erection of his own sarcophagus in the chapel, a sarcophagus which to-day covers the body of Nelson in the crypt of St. Paul's Cathedral. Henry VIII again resumed possession of the Lady Chapel, which seemed to be of ill-omen to those who desired it for a burial-place. His plans for a royal tomb were never completed, and it was left for Queen Victoria to convert it into a Memorial Chapel to the Prince Consort, whose body lies at Frogmore. Beautiful as the exterior of the Albert Memorial Chapel is, it is quite eclipsed by St. George's Chapel, the glory of Windsor, a masterpiece in the Perpendicular style, which ranks second only to Westminster Abbey as a treasure-house of English art and architecture. In the stalls and stall plates of the Knights of the Garter it possesses a unique glory, yet it is known hardly to one in every ten of those who love to visit the Abbey. It contains also the bodies of Edward IV, Henry VI, Henry VIII, and Charles I, while the best craftsmen of the late Middle Ages have left, as a legacy, a noble series of screens in wood, iron, stone, and even bronze work which reaches its perfection in the iron gates built for Edward IV's chantry chapel.

The Kings of England had a tradition to keep up in a palace which was connected with William of Wykeham, who there began his architectural career, and the courtier-poet Geoffrey Chaucer, who was Clerk of the Works, a sinecure which he probably enjoyed more as a courtier than as a poet. The Tudors and Stuarts deserve well enough of the critics, but William and Mary allowed Wren to exercise his taste in surroundings not altogether suited to the architect of the City churches. It is rather surprising that we have to thank George IV for the improvements carried out under the supervision of Sir Jeffrey Wyattville. Not many visitors realize that the Great Tower, originally built in two stories, was carried successfully to its present height only at the beginning of the last century, and we owe to Wyattville the tactful removal of some eighteenth-century incongruities.

WINDSOR

Windsor should draw many visitors because it awakens such different interests. Some are drawn by the romance of battlements, some by the ecclesiastical glories of St. George's Chapel, and some by the splendid furniture, the carvings of Grinling Gibbons, the many paintings of Van Dyck, Rubens, and the great English artists in the State Apartments. However, as the attendance at the National Gallery falls below the attendance at the Zoo, it is not surprising that Windsor's short distance from London should further discourage our contemporaries, who can amuse themselves at home by all the usual methods which do not call for an appreciation of history, art, or architecture.

There should be, nevertheless, a new interest for Englishmen in a castle whose walls are so largely the work of the Norman kings, now that it has been made the *caput honoris* of the reigning house. Throughout English history Windsor has been the castle *par excellence;* and it is in recognition of this that it has become the family seat of the House of Windsor.

WINDSOR CASTLE
(THE NORMAN GATE)

ALNWICK

A FOREIGNER, noting the enthusiasm with which Englishmen visit their old Cathedrals and Abbeys, might imagine a profitable reconstruction of English history from a series of pilgrimages to its mediæval military remains. Certainly there are prehistoric and British earthworks, especially in the English hill-country; there are the Roman forts—the first border-holds of England—dotted along the wall of Hadrian and the Saxon shore; at their highest navigable points many English rivers flow past Danish camps. Castle Hill, at Thetford, may be put down as Anglo-Saxon, while, as the Bayeux Tapestry proves beyond a doubt, Hastings is contemporary in time and identical in situation with the Norman invasion. Why not then see the whole pageant of history in these Norman fortresses, in the adulterine castles raised under Stephen, in the works of that great builder Henry III, and of his son Edward I, Conqueror of Wales? And why not in the Cinque Ports; in Bodiam, a manor house fortified under Richard II for the protection of Hythe in case of a French landing; and in deserted Amberley, raised by the Bishops of Chichester? The chain extends link by link through the Wars of the Roses to the sea-coast forts fostered by Henry VIII and Elizabeth; it includes Peveril, in the Peak district, around which Scott wove his romance of the Stuarts, and Oxford, defended by Prince Rupert; and even—a weak link indeed—the Strawberry Hill Gothic mansions, so typical of the eighteenth century; a chain which did not end with the Martello towers of the Napoleonic wars, for are not English cliffs to-day still crowned by trenches and barbed wire? With these earthworks English warfare returned to its earliest beginnings.

A foreigner with a keen eye to distinguish between true and false would, indeed, derive profit from such a pilgrimage. But he would have to realize that few English castles are faithful witnesses to the past. Of the adulterine castles characteristic of the anarchy of Stephen's reign, hardly one can be identified with certainty to-day—it may be, indeed, that earthworks commonly thought to be British are relics of these very castles. Pontefract, which once was called the Troy of England, is now a heap of rubble in a garden; Colchester, built by the Conqueror against the Danes, has become the shelter for a museum; York and Lincoln are now used as prisons, which, as one writer on the subject naïvely remarks, " naturally bars access to the public "; Peveril has gained a mistaken fame amongst tourists, for Haddon Hall appears to have been the real scene of Scott's novel. Such a man would be wise to concentrate on those castles which preserve or reconstruct their original strength of outline, which indicate their former purpose and importance. And of these castles Alnwick is one.

Although the castle of Alnwick has been rebuilt, it still boasts of the name of Percy, a family as famous in Border literature as the strongholds they maintained; it still stands prepared for a siege as it did in the time of Harry Hotspur, allowing for the improbable event of an army approaching with trebuchets and mangonels; with antiquarian pride the Dukes of Northumberland have restored to it much of the apparatus of defence; while the stone " defenders "—figures of bowmen on the battlements meant to frighten the enemy—still mount guard over the gatehouse. It is, in fact, an excellent example of the creation of a modern country house without prejudice to the form of a mediæval castle.

ALNWICK

Lying on a slight slope from the south bank of the river Aln, the castle was strategically important in its command of the road between Berwick and Newcastle, which made it inevitably a focus of Border warfare. Its known history began soon after the Conquest, with the knowledge that the family of De Vesci was in possession of the site in the reign of Henry I. Eustace FitzJohn, who married into the De Vesci family, is commonly believed to have built the castle. The whole formation of the building points to the date at which he held the barony, with which the innermost gateway and the lower part of the outer curtain wall bear evident traces of identification. So the period of the castle's building may be placed in the first half of the twelfth century.

Throughout its reconstructions—in the fourteenth century, in 1760, and again in 1854—the plan of the castle has not been altered to any great extent. The mound is covered with domestic buildings, and the whole surrounded by a curtain wall making an enclosure which is divided into two wards. FitzJohn probably built the curtain walls, levelled the mound to its present height, and replaced by his shell keep in stone the wooden donjon and palisade, which, together with the domestic buildings within the palisade, formed the earliest castle on this spot. The pure form of a shell keep has been obscured, however, by the present cluster of towers and connecting buildings which evolved as military needs became less pressing than the desire for comfort and splendour.

Still it never lost the character of a shell keep, for, if its possible use as an ultimate refuge had ceased altogether to have weight with the Percys, they would have copied the style of Windsor by building their palace in one of the two wards.

Of the castle's many interesting features one is struck at once by the outer and inner gatehouses. The outer gatehouse,

ALNWICK

fronted by the barbican, projects altogether nearly a hundred feet outside the west curtain. Originally the castle ditch, which passed between barbican and gatehouse, had a loop passing in front of the barbican, so that the gatehouse was protected by two drawbridges and a portcullis, in addition to its flanking rectangular buttresses corbelled out above into oblong turrets containing shelters. An enemy force might well hesitate before attempting to enter here, as the long, narrow passage of the barbican would shepherd an attacking party together like sheep in a pen. The danger of an attempt to turn the flank of the gatehouse by a breach in the curtain wall was met by a series of flanking towers, from which an enemy who did succeed in forcing an entrance to one of the two wards would be assailed in the rear as well as from the towers of the keep. On the north, towards the river, the keep was formerly unprotected by the curtain wall, as though inviting an attack from a quarter more easily defended by the broad ditch and by the natural slope of the river bank, which was artificially scarped. Communications between the outer and inner wards were safeguarded by the middle gate, and the entrance to the keep in the inner ward by a gatehouse, evidently built in the fourteenth century around the gateway which protected the citadel of Eustace FitzJohn. Of this a fine Norman arch remains.

No doubt a lover of romance whose imagination is most easily stirred by the obvious would linger long over the prison chambers in the arches of the gates, complete with underground oubliettes for refractory prisoners, but these were probably used more often as a repository of herrings and salt meat than for despairing captives. More interesting, however—especially to an artist—is the picturesque well within the courtyard of the keep. The hood of the well has the form of three niches within a containing arch. The well shaft rises through the central niche,

ALNWICK

and in the other two are wooden wheels set round with pegs for the hoisting of buckets. Above is a statue of a monk blessing the source, probably an eighteenth-century embellishment. The mediæval architect lavished his ornamentation upon the most necessary features of his building, thereby differing from his modern successor, to whom ornament often appears a means of filling up blank spaces; and this well is a reminder that a siege was not a highly adventurous series of sorties, or of hand-to-hand fighting along the walls, but a test of passive endurance, until either the supplies of food and drink failed the besieged, or the army of the besieger melted away to their fields and flocks.

In all Border warfare Alnwick was one of the strongest fortresses on the English side. In its earliest days, when it could have been little more than a palisaded mound, Malcolm III of Scotland was killed there by an English knight of Robert de Mowbray's levy raised on behalf of William Rufus. Near the Ravine tower in the north-east curtain wall, variations in the masonry mark what is known as the "Bloody Gap," said traditionally to be the position of a breach made by the Scots; but a modern historian, more restrained than the legendmonger, declares that it more probably marks the site of a fallen curtain tower, and as Eustace FitzJohn built the Norman castle some time after the date of this affray, the truth is, unfortunately, on the side of the historian.

Another Scottish monarch met a less dignified fate outside the walls of the castle of FitzJohn. William the Lion had invaded England on behalf of Henry II's rebel sons. He was besieging Alnwick with a small force of 500 knights, while, unknown to him, Odonel de Umfraville, Bernard de Balliol, and other northern barons were advancing to its relief throughout the night, by forced march and in fog.

ALNWICK

Andrew Lang well describes the scene in his history of Scotland :—

"So thick was the air that some were for returning. Balliol, however, insisted on an advance. They passed unseen by Warkworth, then beleaguered by the Scots, and when the cloud lifted found themselves near Alnwick Castle, which was in friendly hands. Thither they rode, when they beheld a party of knights tilting in a meadow. It was like a scene in the 'Morte d'Arthur': the blind advance in an unknown enchanted land, the apparition of the castle above the breaking cloud, the sun shining on the armour of the strange tilting knights. To them the Yorkshire horsemen seemed part of one of their own scattered companies; but when William marked the English cognizances, he, for he was one of the Scottish tilters, rode straight at the ranks of England. His horse was pierced by a spear, and the greatest prize of feudal warfare, a hostile King, with his lords of Norman names, was taken."

William the Lion was ignominiously led away to Newcastle with his legs tied beneath his horse's belly; and the park of Alnwick to-day glories in two monuments marking the downfall of Scottish kings.

The line of de Vesci continued until the end of the thirteenth century, when the castle came into the hands of the Percys, with whose name it is inseparably connected. The history of that family was for centuries the history of England, of Scotland, and, in fact, of France as well, so that in the restorations of the fourteenth century was combined the experience of those who appreciated the necessities of Border warfare with the military knowledge learnt under the Black Prince in France. In the rebellion of the Percys against Henry IV, then, the capture of Alnwick must have been one of the most serious problems which the King was called upon to face. A memory of Harry Hotspur

ALNWICK

lingers in a rectangular projection of the north-east curtain, which is traditionally called Hotspur's Chair; and it may have been one of the hero's favourite posts of observation. But Henry IV was strong enough to take Alnwick in 1405. Hotspur had already fallen at Shrewsbury in 1403, and the Earl of Northumberland shared the violent fate that overtook so many of his family at Bramham Moor in 1408.

The interest of Alnwick lies as much in its past history as in its present state. It began as one of the first outposts set up by the victorious Norman barons against the Scots. It became the possession of a family proud of a name that went back to the early days of the Northmen, a name which was to become an integral part of English literature and history. Alnwick maintains in our day an importance appropriate to its position in the Middle Ages. The struggle for power between the baronage and the monarchy is forgotten, and the castle of the Percys has become their palace.

ALNWICK CASTLE.

ARUNDEL

SALARINO described to the merchant of Venice the ocean

> where your argosies with portly sail,—
> Like signiors and rich burghers on the flood,
> Or, as it were, the pageants of the sea,—
> Do overpeer the petty traffickers,
> That curtsy to them and do them reverence.

One is tempted to transpose that metaphor to Arundel. The poor little houses of the town are in a perpetual attitude of reverent humility at the foot of the great towers which overshadow them. At Richmond or at Norwich, after all, the signiors and rich burghers, the castle towers, still overpeer the petty traffickers which line the streets below, but there is no curtsying; the castles are lordless, and the towns have a commercial importance of their own. Arundel, on the other hand, renders almost feudal homage to the Dukes of Norfolk. Indeed, the town seems to have no other reason for existence to-day—although it is justifiably proud of its past traditions—than to provide servants for the estate and accommodation for the thousands of tourists who come to visit the castle.

Roger de Montgomery was the first to build a castle at Arundel soon after the Conquest. The reference in Domesday to a *castrum* there in the time of Edward the Confessor has been shown to mean the fortifications of the town, but the earthworks outside the castle walls prove that the place was fortified in early times. Even if there were no such evidence one might assume it to have been fortified, for Arundel was of outstanding

ARUNDEL

military importance throughout the Dark Ages and the Middle Ages.

The castle is built upon a spur of the downs commanding the River Arun at a point where there has always been a bridge. Where there is a bridge there is a road, where there is a river there is an avenue of attack from the sea, and where the river passes through the downs there is a gap through which armies can march inland. That is the importance of Arundel, but the lines of mediæval communication made that importance even greater. Arundel held not a bridge, but *the* bridge over the Arun.

In the early history of England, much more than in our day, rivers were used for commerce. Consequently, bridges were not constructed over the mouths of rivers, but at the point where ocean-going vessels could discharge their cargoes nearest to the seats of trade. In Sussex especially, where a number of small rivers parallel to one another opened the country to invasion, and where there were no coastwise roads (for the roads ran from bridge to bridge some miles inland) it was difficult to concentrate an army to repel an invasion. Local conditions such as these made the importance of Arundel, as of Bramber or Lewes. Arundel commanded an essential road at a point vital to the economic and military life of the district. Only recently have bridges at Littlehampton, Shoreham, and Newhaven linked together the coastal roads of Sussex.

Roger de Montgomery contributed sixty ships to the Norman fleet, commanded the centre at Senlac, and became lord of Sussex. Later he was Earl of Shrewsbury, and the family of the Norman adventurer left their name upon the map of Wales in the county where the ruins of their great castle may be seen. At Arundel Roger built a stockaded stronghold with a mound and court. Almost certainly the second court, which gave

ARUNDEL

Arundel the same plan as Windsor, was part of the original design, but it is possible to consider this a later addition, for very little of the Norman work can be identified at Arundel, which has been restored and rebuilt with great care in recent years.

The castle extends its length from north-west to south-east. The long eastern wall is straight and uninterrupted, but the western curtain bends inward at about the middle where it crosses the ditch and climbs the mound to the wall of the keep. That is to say, a portion of the wall of the shell-keep at the summit of the mound faces the field, and the ditch below the mound becomes a part of the main ditch running around the northern end of the castle. Within the enclosure the mound forms the division between the two wards, leaving a narrow space from the edge of the inner ditch to the east curtain. Probably there were never any buildings in the upper ward to the north; this was used as an enclosure for cattle and horses.

The gatehouse, just south of the keep, gives entrance to the lower ward, around three sides of which are grouped the imposing buildings erected chiefly by the late Duke. The basement of the range on the south is partly Norman work. Of the military remains, the keep, a portion of the gatehouse, and the lower half of the Bevis tower in the upper ward are also Norman.

An account of Arundel's history is necessary for an understanding of the castle as it appears at present. Arundel was lost to the family of Montgomery after it had been enjoyed for a time by Roger's son, Robert de Bellesme, who supported Robert of Normandy against Henry I. Henry blockaded the castle with portable wooden towers, and before long the garrison asked for a truce that they might obtain permission to surrender from their lord in Shropshire. The permission was

ARUNDEL

granted, and the besieged were only too glad to march out of the castle, which reverted to the Crown.

Henry's widow, Adela of Louvain, brought Arundel in marriage to William de Albini, the Norfolk landowner who built the keep at Castle Rising, and the ancestor of the present Duke of Norfolk. Adela's brother, Joscelin, was an ancestor of the ducal house of Northumberland. Joscelin was given the domain of Petworth by William de Albini " since which," says Camden, " the posterity of that Joscelin, who took the name of Percy [upon his marriage to Agnes, the heiress of the Percys], have ever possessed it, a family certainly very ancient and noble, the male representatives of Charlemagne, more direct than the Dukes of Guise, who pride themselves on that account."

It is a curious encounter in the bypaths of history to find the two eldest ducal houses of England claimed as the representatives of Charlemagne's line to the exclusion of the French nobility. It is equally curious to find among the descendants of Charlemagne (through Adela of Louvain) two of England's most unhappy queens—Anne Boleyn and Katherine Howard.

William de Albini was chief butler or cup-bearer of the Duchy of Normandy. His descendants, the hereditary Earls Marshal of England, retain the honour, and when a new monarch drinks the health of his liege subjects at the coronation banquet the golden goblet is the perquisite of the Duke of Norfolk.

Adela spent long periods at Arundel. In 1139 she gave refuge to the Empress Matilda, although she held herself neutral in the struggles between Stephen and Matilda. The latter immediately raised his siege of Marlborough, and blockaded Arundel, demanding the surrender of Matilda. But he did not press the attack. According to one account he chivalrously recognized Adela's claim that she was sheltering the daughter of Henry, not the enemy of Stephen. Another version is that

Stephen felt Arundel to be impregnable, and by allowing Matilda to escape to the Earl of Gloucester at Bristol he would have all his opponents shut up together in one part of the country. At all events, he allowed Matilda safe conduct from Sussex.

The great-granddaughter of William de Albini brought Arundel to her husband, John Fitz Alan of Clun, in Shropshire. The Fitz Alan line continued until 1580, when Arundel passed by marriage again to the family of Howard, Dukes of Norfolk.

It cannot be said that Arundel had an eventful military history in the Middle Ages, despite its position of importance. The wars of the seventeenth century proved more destructive for the castle. There were occasions when artillery failed before walls built for the defence of mail-clad knights. Arundel may be cited as a good illustration of Shakespeare's imagery—

> The strongest castle, tower, and town,
> The golden bullet beats it down.

In 1643 Waller captured the castle with the loss of only one man. In Waller's absence, however, the Royalists under the command of Lord Hopton retook town and castle after a three days' siege, but within a fortnight Waller again appeared fully prepared for a lengthy investiture. He planted cannon on the church tower to batter the walls while his musketeers raked the battlements until the keep was a ruin and the domestic buildings shattered to pieces. As usual the wits were among the Royalist party. In an attempt to disguise a shortage of provisions, they gravely offered to give the Puritans beef and mutton in exchange for sack, tobacco, cards, and dice. Of course, the Roundheads had no cards to give away, but they thankfully accepted some live oxen let down from the walls by the garrison as a rather

ARUNDEL

transparent advertisement of their superfluous provisions. Shortly afterwards the garrison surrendered, to the number of about a thousand; they were made prisoners of war. The Commonwealth slighted the castle to complete the work already more than half accomplished by Waller's cannon.

Not until 1791 did the Dukes of Norfolk begin the work of restoration, which was continued to the end of the nineteenth century, when the buildings were practically constructed anew and the defences restored. Much that was capable of restoration, the chapel, for example, has been replaced by modern buildings. But the new chapel in the Early English style is entirely admirable, and no visitor to the great hall or to the library can feel that the restorations are incongruous to the traditions of the castle.

Probably the castle besieged by Henry I was defended by palisades, and the buildings in stone were begun by him when he had possession of the place. The oldest existing portion is the inner gatehouse which contains dungeons reminiscent of the inner gateway at Alnwick. It also covers the approach to the keep along the top of the curtain wall running up the mound. Richard FitzAlan, in the thirteenth century, constructed a more elaborate outer gatehouse with two towers fronting the drawbridge, so that the whole work is not unlike the barbican at Warwick, the passage 40 feet in length being defended by gate and portcullis.

The shell-keep probably dates from the time of Henry II. In this type of keep the rooms were built against the inner walls, leaving an open space in the middle. They were, no doubt, of wood, and have disappeared, but a musty cellar or storehouse excavated from the space in the centre still remains. Originally the keep was entered by a Norman door in the south face. Evidently the approach was too easy, and there was no protection afforded to the well on the slope of the mound near the curtain, so two towers were built to cover the entrance. The smaller tower contains the well, and the larger tower encloses the keep entrance underneath a small oratory dedicated to Saint Martin. An enemy who had captured the gatehouse would have short shrift if he found himself upon the uncovered curtain wall at the foot of those well-protected towers.

The keep and its towers were repaired by the late duke, as well as the machinery for working the portcullis in the entrance tower. The Roundhead policy of dismantling the great castles of the country is now thoroughly reversed, at Arundel at least, and the visitor finds an equal interest in the walls and turrets of the upper ward, and the books and paintings of the palace overlooking the River Arun.

ARUNDEL CASTLE.

BAMBURGH

THERE are in England many towns that have grown up around feudal castles, but Bamburgh is unique as a fortress upon the site of which was once " the mistress of the cities of Britain." It might almost be said that, with the building of the Norman castle the glory of Bamburgh departed. For upon this volcanic rock jutting into the North Sea was a British stronghold, Dinguardi, which became the capital of the Northumbrian kingdom, Bernicia. Bebbanburh, as it was called by the Angles, held sway over the mingled fortunes of Bernicia and Deira, now the glory of a victorious nation and again the impregnable refuge of a broken people. The history of Bamburgh in that period mirrors the defeat of the Britons, the savagery of pagan Mercia under Penda, the extension of Wessex under Alfred's house, and the low Danish ships driving in from the east.

This barren cliff-top, described by one chronicler as about the size of two fields, was yet the subject of a lamentation worthy of Jerusalem. " She has exchanged her ancient sabbaths," wrote Reginald of Durham, " for shame and desolation. The crowds that flocked to her festivals are represented by a few herdsmen. The pleasures her dignity afforded us are now no more."

Indeed, there was an end to Ilium. At some period, which it is impossible to fix, the inhabitants of the shrunken capital built a new, inglorious Bamburgh, outside the enceinte of what is now the castle.

This " corner of Northumberland defended on all sides by the sea and the marshes," was the last refuge of the Conqueror's enemies in the North. Fortified as it was, even then possibly with stone walls, careful strategy was needed to make it surrender, and he paid Bamburgh the compliment, shared only by Durham and York, of leaving it untouched when he laid waste Northumbria in 1070. A soldier's eye saw the value of the site, and the history of Bamburgh as a castle began.

Often enough, of course, the Normans used existing fortifications until the opportunity arose to build after their own manner —an opportunity which in some cases did not present itself until the twelfth century. All that we know certainly about the date of its building is that the keep was an addition to a completed castle; not, as in the case of the White Tower, or the keep at Dover, a nucleus around which concentric fortifications were afterwards built. The keep was erected by Henry II in 1163, ten years before that of Newcastle.

The plan of Bamburgh is long and narrow, with its north-eastern side fronting the sea. On such a site there was no question of throwing up a mound to make a fortress of the mound and bailey type. Instead, three wards were built. The inner or eastern ward contained the halls, kitchens, vaults and living quarters with the twelfth-century chapel of St. Oswald, of which the carefully-preserved foundations now remain. The keep at the eastern end of the middle ward has unfortunately lost some of its aspect as a fortress owing to an eighteenth-century effort to convert it into a private residence. This necessitated the piercing of the walls with large, unsightly windows, and the reorganization of its exterior plan.

In the basement of the keep there is to be found a well, described in Anglo-Saxon times as " most sweet to the taste, most pure to see, which has been excavated out of the solid rock with marvellous labour." Despite its importance to the castle it was lost sight of during the sixteenth century and only discovered by accident in 1770. Its depth is 150 ft.—the actual height of the rock above sea level at that point—which is truly " of a marvellus grett dypnes " for such early work. Another marvel in early times was the flight of steps cut out of the solid rock at the lower end of the castle to the north. Examination proves that these became the mediæval postern steps, but the indiscriminate renovators of the eighteenth century had no compunction in destroying them. In general, at Bamburgh, although much is ancient, the visitor must approach warily each " Norman " door and " mediæval " tower.

Bamburgh has had to stand the test of several sieges, but its impregnability was a byword so long as gunpowder was unknown. William Rufus, who besieged Robert de Mowbray there in 1095, was reduced to blockading tactics. He threw up a temporary castle, which he nicknamed " Malvoisin," and which was so near the walls that William is said to have suffered from the taunts of the beleaguered garrison. And, in the end, Mowbray's fall was due, not to a breach in the walls or to the failure of food supplies, but to his own capture after the sortie he made to get possession of Newcastle.

In effect, this was a victory for the throne that only increased the reputation of Bamburgh. For William was wise enough to imprison Mowbray, suppress his earldom, and make Bamburgh a royal fortress. Thenceforward it was governed by Constables, who were royal nominees.

Nevertheless, its very strength as a mediæval fortress can be looked at from another aspect. The object of the mediæval castle builder was to construct a place of passive strength, easily defended, and it can be said that, had six men of their time possessed modern rifles, they could have held the castle against all comers. As a royal stronghold, the history of Bamburgh was well documented, and these documents describe a line of incompetent and dishonest Constables, a castle largely ruinous and desperately devoid of ammunition. Three great statesmen, Henry I, Henry II, and Hubert de Burgh, devoted their attention to Bamburgh, but the state of the castle at other times is fairly shown by an inventory of 1248, in which we are told that the garrison could boast only of two hauberks, three doublets, two helmets and eight iron caps " all old and valueless." There were thirteen small ballistæ—no more than crossbows—and ten barrels of " quarrels " for them. And, carefully recorded like treasures of great price, are these tools: two crowbars and one broken iron hammer, six axes and one pickaxe, three worthless coppers in the furnace, three old brass pots, three worthless dishes and a gridiron. On another occasion all the provisions to be found were: four casks of sour wine, a pipe of Greek wine, " no better," one jar full of honey and another with some honey in it.

Again consider the structure of the castle. A Constable in the time of Edward III reported extensive ruins: the lead was decayed and the beams were rotting; the tower was threatened with ruin; the stone roofs of the Davytoure and of the Belletoure had been carried right off by a tempest; all other parts of the castle were in great decay. Yet even in this ruined state, Scottish attacks were beaten off for three months during the year 1328, with what seems to us the small loss of five ballistæ, a bucketful of bolts, the one bow the castle possessed, and all of its five sheaves of arrows. Evidently mediæval castles were not always the perfect strongholds they were represented to be. Or rather the science of siegecraft, in England at any rate, was largely undeveloped.

In this connection though, it must not be overlooked that the garrison was aided by the services of the crown tenants. Few sums of money are put down for repairs in the Rolls of the Exchequer.

BAMBURGH

In fact, repairs might almost have been a means of revenue, for in 1170 the Thane of Hepple was fined five marks for refusing to lend his assistance. Francis Grose conjectured that the small stones used for the tower must have been brought on the backs of men and horses from a quarry three miles away.

Although Bamburgh lacks in its history some of the dignity of Warwick or of Arundel, both seats of feudal dynasties, it is a place

> Where Sultan after Sultan with his pomp
> Abode his destined Hour and went his way.

It is, indeed, a commentary on English history, the strength or the weakness of its kings. Thus the powerful Hubert de Burgh proceeded to Bamburgh, accompanied by Brito the Balister, and his eighteen comrades. In the same year the castle was visited by the young Henry III with an insignificant retinue. There is an echo of Edward I's Welsh victories, when we find two princes from Wales confined in the castle, while Edward II is shown characteristically making a pretext of imprisoning Piers Gaveston at Bamburgh to secure him from his enemies. After the Battle of Neville's Cross, David Bruce, " who called himself King of Scotland," was brought to Bamburgh and, ten years afterwards, Edward III there completed the final convention with Edward Balliol for the latter's surrender of the Scottish Crown. The strong John of Gaunt restored it, and Harry Hotspur was made Constable as a reward for his share in the dethronement of Richard II.

Bamburgh's most intimate connection with royalty was a tragic one; the unavailing refuge of Margaret of Anjou, it sheltered the unhappy Henry VI for some months, finally endured a famous siege, and, sorely battered, owned itself defeated by the new artillery. After Towton, Margaret of Anjou, assisted by Lancastrians and French mercenaries, made two attempts to maintain a *pied-à-terre* for her husband in that part of Northumberland guarded by Bamburgh, Alnwick, and Dunstanburgh. But she had to cope with Warwick the King Maker, and at one time was so closely blockaded at Bamburgh that she was forced to escape to a storm-bound French fleet, and finally reached Berwick in a fishing smack. In the meantime, the garrison, after eating their horses, surrendered to Warwick. Nevertheless, within four months, " by false collusion and treason," Margaret again had possession of the castle, and with her was Henry VI. She failed to take Norham, was chased back to Bamburgh by Warwick, and so escaped again with her son to secure French aid, leaving Henry VI in safety. Probably the real security of Henry's position lay, not so much in stone ramparts, as in Warwick's doubt whether it would be to his own best interests to crush the Lancastrians too effectively. He withdrew southward, leaving Henry undisputed monarch of a little kingdom. To his liege subjects of Alnwick and Dunstanburgh the royal commands were issued; even upon the citizens of Edinburgh was conveyed a charter granting trading privileges with the principality in Henry's possession, until at last the danger of French intrigue forced Edward to march north and scatter Lancastrian court and kingdom to the winds of heaven.

Bamburgh, whence Henry had been assisted to escape, sustained a siege which was a strange mixture of mediæval pageantry and modern science. The Warwick Herald and the King's Chester Herald were despatched to demand the surrender from the Constable " and other that held his rebellious opinion." But he " had clearly determined within himself to live or die in the Castle." So the heralds departed after delivering a final warning against the destruction of the castle : " the which the King, our most sovereign lord, hath so greatly in favour seeing it marcheth so nigh his ancient enemies of Scotland, he specially desireth to have it whole, unbroken with ordinance; if ye suffer one great gun laid unto the wall and be shot and prejudice the wall, it shall cost you the chieftain's head; and so proceeding for every gun shot to the last head of any person within the place."

So " Newe-castel," " London," and the King's brazen gun, ' Dijon," came into play. They so " betyde " the place that great stones flew into the sea, and Dijon shot through Sir Ralph Grey's chamber oftentimes. The castle capitulated, and Sir Ralph Grey was led to Doncaster for execution, one of the chief counts against him being that he had " withstood and made fences against the King's Majesty and his lieutenant, the worthy Lord of Warwick, as appeareth by the strokes of the great guns in the king's wall of his castle of Bamburgh."

This siege gave Bamburgh a certain fame which it might otherwise have lacked. It is widely known, not as a royal town, nor as a castle merely, but as *the* castle upon whose walls was triumphantly demonstrated the supremacy of artillery. So historians have said, forgetting that the growth of common law destroyed more of the feudal strongholds than did ever " London," " Newe-castel," or " Dijon "; forgetting also that Basing House, a fortified manor, held out against the improved cannons of a later century. The real interest of the siege and of Bamburgh is a more human one. The sight of that long-stretching sea-wall and the water-gate is a reminder of Queen Margaret bravely setting out to prepare a new attack on the usurper, of Henry in vigil for the help that never came to him on earth. There are memories here of kings in plenty, and anyone who is interested in such things will find a fount of interest in the history of the Anglian royal town—of Aidan, Cuthbert, Oswald of the Fair Hand, and Queen Bebba, whose name was given to the spot.

Even the enthusiastic renovations of the eighteenth century

BAMBURGH

may be forgiven to the trustees of Lord Crewe, Bishop of Durham, whose aim it was to make the castle into a refuge for shipwrecked sailors. Lord Armstrong, the present owner, has done much to restore the characteristic features of its earlier history.

Bamburgh as a target for those strange new guns is of minor importance. It stands to-day a monument of men, not of things. It held the border of two nations that are now one on behalf of a monarchy that now rules an Empire.

BAMBURGH CASTLE.

CAERPHILLY

CAERPHILLY in Glamorganshire has no great reputation among British castles. It is a hollow shell without sufficient historical or human interest to draw large numbers of tourists. Nevertheless, with the exception of Windsor it was the largest of our castles in area, as it was also the first and finest of the concentric type in these islands. As at Kenilworth, the imagination receives little assistance in reconstructing the mediæval fortress. Its scheme was one of islands protected by the lakes they stood in, but the water has been drained away. Long ago every trace of metalwork and woodwork was removed; gunpowder was used either to quarry its stones or to destroy its military value, and the towers without battlements, the buildings without roofs, present a mass of walls in which it is difficult to detect a concentric, or indeed any, plan.

Caerphilly was a Marcher castle, an outpost of the lords of Glamorgan to protect Cardiff and the coastal plain from the forays of unbeaten Welshmen in the Brecon hills. It lay on a knoll in the plain between two rivers, the Rhymney and the Taff, the knoll jutting out like a peninsula into swampy ground between two small rivulets on their way to join the larger streams.

Perhaps the tradition is correct, that this was the site of a Welsh stronghold, Senghennydd, but it was Gilbert de Clare, third Earl of Gloucester and Hertford, who built the concentric castle there at the end of the reign of Henry III. For some time de Clare had quarrelled with Llewelyn over this land, and the castle could hardly have been half-completed before Llewelyn laid siege to it, and would only withdraw when the King himself intervened. After that, the great strength of the castle was really wasted, for immediately after it was erected Edward conquered and fortified North Wales, so that Caerphilly sank to a position of the second rank. The attacks it suffered were not launched by Welshmen against the English, but in the hurly-burly of rebellion and civil war.

The plan of Caerphilly is difficult to describe, owing to its complexity and its refinements. Its gravel peninsula projected eastward into a swamp shaped not unlike a horseshoe, and divided the low ground into two parts. The damming of two rivulets turned the swamp into a lake, and the peninsula, by two cross-cuts, became two islands. The inmost island, facing the arch of the horseshoe, held the main buildings of the castle. Between the castle and the root of the peninsula, and connected with them by drawbridges, was formed a horn-work or platform, its banks surrounded by ramparts. But the main approach to the castle was from the east, and the whole eastern side of the lake was protected by a long straight curtain wall, equally a barbican and a fortified dam upon which the lake system depended. This east front was an impregnable defence. It had towers at either end, those on the south across the rivulet to form a *tête-du-pont*. It was defended by bastions and buttresses, by a strong gatehouse, and by a broad moat along its front. Before the gatehouse, in the middle of the moat, was a stone pier; and the two sections of the drawbridge met and rested upon this. The gatehouse gave access to the platform behind the eastern curtain wall, and from there to the castle buildings was a third drawbridge. In addition to these defences, there was a thin tongue of land curving from the hornwork towards the east front, with which it was brought into connection by a wall.

The defences of Caerphilly, then, consisted of an outer moat and outer wall, a north and south lake, an inner moat, the hornwork, and the two wards of the actual castle buildings. In addition, to the north of the castle is a well-defended redoubt, but this must date from the Stuart wars. The details of Caerphilly's fortifications were well thought out. The castle mill was on the platform behind the east front, and in the middle ward was a large water tank, probably used as a *vivarium* for the supply of fish.

CAERPHILLY CASTLE.

The eastern or Grand Front of Caerphilly was, in itself, a very complete line of defence. The end towers prevented it from being outflanked, and protected that part of the curtain which controlled the river waters flowing through it. The gatehouse controlled the whole line, while the pier before it did duty as a barbican. But in addition, the wall 20 ft. high and 6 ft. thick, which connected the bank of the inner moat with the eastern front, also cut the latter into two halves at a point just north of the gatehouse. If either end of the eastern front were captured, the rest could hold out by itself. This division of the front allowed also for a narrow postern at that point, to which entrance could only be gained by boat.

The eastern front and its system of defence is generally taken as the outer ward of the castle. The middle ward—the outer ward of the castle buildings—was surrounded by a low wall with bastions at the angles. It possessed its own turreted gatehouses, east and west, and the kitchens were housed in a tower in this ward, adjacent to the south wall of the inner ward where the hall was situated.

The inner ward was surrounded by a lofty curtain wall with four corner towers, and again two strong gatehouses gave access to it. Against the south side were the hall, a beautiful building in the decorated style, attributed to Hugh le Despenser, which is one of the better preserved parts of the castle; and at either end of the hall were the chapel and the dwelling apartments.

The striking feature of Caerphilly was the provision for easy egress, but formidable obstacles were thrown in the way of any one seeking to effect an entrance. While an enemy was attacking the main gateway in the eastern front, he could easily be taken in the rear by a party from the western gateway or from the postern in the *tête-du-pont*.

It cannot be said that all this castle was built at one time, but it is obvious that it was constructed according to the original plan. Probably the military parts of the castle buildings were first completed, but the architects must have provided for the defences on the eastern front and the horn-work, or else the position would have been untenable. The complicated system of defence is a single whole, probably the product of one mind.

Caerphilly had no great part in history, partly because it was not the seat of a feudal barony, but merely an appendage to the

CAERPHILLY

lords of Cardiff. Through marriage the castle came into the hands of the Despensers; during 1326 King Edward II, fleeing from the Queen and her confederates, was twice at Caerphilly, which was afterwards besieged by Isabel, as we learn from a pardon made out to John de Felton for withstanding the Queen and Prince Edward at the castle of " Kerfilly." But any historical references to the castle are incidental. In some way it was connected with Owen Glendower at a later period; a royal writ, on the one hand, commits Caerphilly to the keeping of Constantia, Lady de Despenser, for the suppression of Glendower; but, on the other hand, tradition (though wrongly) attributes the famous leaning tower of the inner ward to the period when Glendower held and destroyed the castle.

Leland, in his Itinerary, speaks of " Caerfilly Castelle sette amonge marshes, wher be walles of a wonderful thickness and tower kept up for prisoners. . . ."

The destruction of Caerphilly was already begun when Leland wrote, and the story of its spoliation, so far as it can be pieced together, is a parable of how closely the lives of men are connected with the buildings they erect. About three-quarters of a mile from the castle is the ruin of a manor house, the Ffanvawr, of which now only the outer walls and a dovecote remain; but much of the hewn stone built into its walls is obviously from the castle. The manor house was built in Tudor times, and it belonged to the family of Lewis, whose ancestors had been the native lords of Senghennydd long before Caerphilly Castle was built. And there is a document dating from the time of Henry VIII giving to the family of Lewis the right " to take out and carie awaie from the within namyd castle of Caerfilley suche and so many of the stones thereof as . . . shall seeme convenient and mete for the necessearie buildings of the saide Thomas Lewys at his house called the Vann."

CAERPHILLY

So we may suppose that the old enemies of Caerphilly at last despoiled it. They took away the fireplaces and the woodwork, the lead and iron, they threw down the towers with gunpowder and dislodged their stones, for the building of a peaceful manor house where the old Welsh family would live when the Marcher lords were the forgotten enemies of the past. There is almost a touch of Russian fatalism in the rivalry of these stone buildings, both now broken and in decay.

CARISBROOKE, CORFE, AND PORCHESTER

THE famous saying, "They little know of England who only England know," is less an epigram than a platitude. It may be true that England's greatest achievements are to be found on seven seas and five continents, but it is even more obvious that the ordinary Englishman knows less than a little about his own country. Its castles are a case in point. The names of some are household words, others are hardly known at all; and those that are forgotten are often the most ancient or the most impressive, whether in ruins or in repair. To the thousands who will boast that their country possesses Warwick, the names of Warkworth, Hurstmonceaux, Raglan, and Bodiam, may be empty sounds.

The castles which are so little known, however, are often enough those that have played small part in English history. Their towers may be majestic, their ruins striking, but any historic importance they possess is due to one spectacular incident or qualification. Porchester, for instance, in the later years of Roman Britain, protected the vast harbour at the end of Stane Street; Carisbrooke was the "narrow chase" of Charles Stuart's captivity; and Corfe is spoken of as the place where the young Saxon King Edward was murdered.

None the less, throughout the Middle Ages the harbour now called Portsmouth was of vital importance and necessarily well defended. The Roman system of roads connected it with London by way of Chichester and the Weald as well as through Southampton and Winchester. The Norman invasion magnified

CARISBROOKE, CORFE, AND PORCHESTER

tenfold every motive that existed in the time of the Saxon isolation for communication with the Continent, and no harbour to which a Roman road still led could remain unprotected or unused. The Norman rulers also made such effective defensive measures that we can imagine the Danish pirates spirited, rather than frightened away, from the scene of English history.

That is the *raison d'être* of Colchester keep, and partly of the Tower of London. Nearer to our subject, Farnham Castle had some of its yearly dues remitted on account of its duty of defence against the Vikings; and Porchester also protected its harbour from these attacks. Besides, as a royal castle, it was a resting-place for kings on their continental journeys, particularly when Winchester rather than London was the capital of the Angevin Empire, and later during the intermittent French wars.

PORCHESTER CASTLE.

Obviously the Normans did not adapt the walls of Porchester to their uses because they found them standing; for Richborough, without the harbour it once guarded, was neglected by them. But Porchester was in a splendid military position on a tongue of land projecting into the harbour, so that two of the walls of the square Roman fort were washed by the sea, and at a short distance from the landward walls a broad ditch—perhaps the remains of an earlier fortification—cut across the approaches. Allowing for necessary repairs and a few mediæval alterations the walls enclosing the outer ward to-day are of the original Roman workmanship in flint concrete, with occasional projecting bastions. On the eastern curtain two bastions flank the mediæval water-gate (for it was part of the strength of Porchester that it could easily be relieved or provisioned from the harbour), but the south-east corner bastion has been undermined by sea-water, and the north-western corner is occupied by the keep.

In this angle of the Roman fort a castle grew up in the twelfth century, and it was kept in repair as a protection for Portsmouth Harbour until the end of the Hundred Years' War. After that it lapsed to private tenants, who occasionally leased it back to the Crown, when it was wanted as a place of internment for prisoners of war. So the history of Porchester is less glorious than instructive.

The first documentary mention of a castle at Porchester occurs in a grant of 1153, but as the royal treasure was removed there for a time in 1163, we can imagine that it was already of some strength. The keep, of which the lower part appears to be of the early twelfth century, confirms this documentary evidence of its strength. It has none of the domestic graces that make the White Tower at London as much a palace as a citadel, and military requirements weighed more heavily with its builders. The keep dominated the castle and the plain in which it stood. It consisted of a basement and two floors to which (as at Corfe) two further stories were added at a later period. It had a forebuilding leading to the second story, from which a spiral staircase gave the only access to the basement; and while there are some good windows in the upper part of the present keep, the original building must have been remarkable for its dark and musty interior.

The only other remaining Norman work is the curtain wall of the inner ward, forming a square bailey in the corner of the original enclosure. The domestic buildings ranged along the western and southern walls of the inner ward include a hall built by Richard II, the royal living rooms, and a building which may have been used for the Exchequer; but the buildings on the eastern side of the ward were erected in seventeenth-century Gothic by Sir Thomas Cornwallis.

In the south-eastern corner of the outer ward is a Norman church built in the time of Henry I for a royal foundation as the priory church of a new house of Austin Canons. For some reason or other the site was found to be inconvenient by the Canons, who abandoned it, but the church was kept well enough repaired. In a petition to Queen Anne it is stated that in the reign of Charles II the church, having been used to keep prisoners of war, " was by their means set on fire and for the greater part ruined," but however great the damage, it has since been made good.

Porchester Castle was a silent eyewitness of the conflict between Church and State in the twelfth and thirteenth centuries. It was there that the Bishop of Evreux met Henry II to mediate between him and St. Thomas à Becket over the constitutions of Clarendon, and eight years later Henry found himself again at Porchester, publicly declaring his innocence in the matter of the Archbishop's murder, in the presence of the Papal Legates. King John, that much-travelled monarch, was often at Porchester. He was there when the Pope's interdict was promulgated in England. But John must be chiefly remembered by his missive to the barons of the Exchequer, " that we lent our brother, the Earl of Salisbury, at Porchester, ten shillings to play."

After the reign of Elizabeth the castle was used chiefly as a prison. Norden, in 1609, said the castle was then ruined " by reason the leade hathe been cutt and imbezeled." The hall he described as " verye fayer and spacious," the other rooms being " maine spacious but dark and malincolie," and he wanted one tower lowered " because it annoyeth the reste of the howse by reflexe of the chimneye smoake," which appears to be a simple method of curing the smoke evil, though it would hardly commend itself to Londoners to-day. But Porchester was not to degenerate quietly into a useless ruin. It was filled with Dutchmen after Blake's sea victories, and with Frenchmen during the Napoleonic wars. It is almost incredible that about five thousand Frenchmen were stowed away there at one time.

The suggestion that Porchester should then be used as a naval hospital produced a protest, which was a curious comment upon the lot of the French prisoners, but perhaps the report of 1855 was a slightly jaundiced view. " A building ruinous and falling to pieces," it ran, " badly ventilated . . . badly lighted, the site low, bleak, with miles of exposed mud before it, difficult of access, and containing within its walls the parish church and churchyard, there could scarcely be chosen a less desirable place for the proposed hospital."

The writers of that report on Roman walls and Norman keep were practical but surely very unimaginative people.

Carisbrooke also goes back to very early beginnings, and it has been brought to a more picturesque decline. The site of the castle was anciently the chief stronghold on the Isle of Wight, and fortified in all probability by the Jutes. Some, who place their simple faith in the most disputed passages of the Anglo-Saxon Chronicle, identify Carisbrooke as the " Wihtgarasburh," where Cynric and Cerdic defeated the islanders in 530, and where Wihtgar himself was buried.

Certainly the chalk spur on which Carisbrooke stands is a natural position for defence, and the castle buildings cut right across well-defined earthworks of an earlier date. This was the form of the Conqueror's castle, which was probably surrounded by wooden stockades with some stone buildings.

After the Conquest the lordship of the island with the castle of Carisbrooke was alternately vested in short-lived or rebellious families and resumed by the Crown. The Fitz Osborns, for instance, were enfeoffed at the Conquest and deprived in 1078 for complicity in the conspiracy of Ralph Guader. The de Redvers, to whom the grant was made by Henry I, built most of the stone part of the castle. Baldwin de Redvers, an adherent of Matilda, raised " a castle stately, built of hewn stone and strengthened by great fortifications," against Stephen; but the wells ran dry, and he submitted without putting his work to the test of war. In 1293 the line ended in a woman, Isabel de Fortibus—a very capable woman, herself an active builder, who left her mark on the castle. After her death the castle was held by the monarchy for long periods, and its military works were kept in repair until late in the seventeenth century.

The early works were probably begun by William Fitz Osborn and carried on by the Conqueror. They dictated the form of the present castle by constructing an artificial mound of chalk rubble at the north-east corner of an oblong bailey enclosed by high chalk banks. The chapel of St. Nicholas, near the centre of the enclosure (restored in 1904 in memory of King Charles) was in existence at the time of the Domesday survey. The domestic buildings were ranged along the north bank, and the defences were probably wooden stockades until the de Redvers replaced them by stone walls. It was in this early castle that William the Conqueror personally arrested his half-brother, Odo of Bayeux, Earl of Kent, and sent him prisoner to Rouen, with the successful quibble that he laid hands, not on the consecrated Bishop, but on the rebellious Earl.

CARISBROOKE, CORFE, AND PORCHESTER

History, however, moved slowly on this small island, dwelling apart from the larger world of mediæval England. Carisbrooke only endured one siege, and that in the late fourteenth century, so that the improvement in its fortifications went on undisturbed. The de Redvers built the polygonal shell keep on the mound, approached by a flight of seventy-one steps from the bailey, and constructed stone curtain walls around the bailey. The original Norman entrance on the west side was considerably altered and strengthened by subsequent lords and governors of the castle, being ultimately defended by a narrow passage containing three archways with portcullises, fronted by a gatehouse with towers. The fourteenth century is a late period in the history of English castellation, but these and other improvements (such as the forebuilding added to the keep) were begun in 1334 " by command of the King for fear of invasion of the island," and the King's fears were not ungrounded. In 1377 the French landed in force, destroyed the town of Francheville (where Newtown now stands) and besieged Carisbrooke. They were beaten off, some say the invaders were annihilated; but at least the brief military history of the castle was not inglorious.

The next scare was the Armada. Carisbrooke was hastily prepared for defence by a levy *en masse* of the islanders, but the danger passed by. It was after the defeat of the Armada that Elizabeth called on the engineer Gianibelli, who made a long outer line of defence with bastions and ravelines according to the latest methods of warfare, to protect the castle.

Jerome, Earl of Portland, was dismissed from the Governorship of Carisbrooke as a Royalist and Papist, in 1642, to be replaced by one Colonel Hammond, and Parliament spent £246 in repairs to its walls and gatehouses in 1658. It was to this castle, so favoured by Parliament, and to its rebel governor, that Charles was persuaded to entrust himself, rather unwillingly,

CARISBROOKE, CORFE, AND PORCHESTER

when he fled from Hampton Court. He was held at first in the Constable's lodgings, but, on his attempting to escape, when he found hospitality a disguised captivity, his quarters were removed to a small chamber between the hall and the north curtain. He again attempted to escape, but he desisted just in time, for there is a suspicion that the good Hammond, having got wind of the venture, was waiting outside to shoot him in the very act of escaping. Despite these associations with their father, the Council of State, in 1650, sent the young Duke of Gloucester and the Princess Elizabeth to Carisbrooke, where they were housed in the chambers Charles had occupied; and there the tragic little Princess declined and died, being found with her head pillowed on her Bible, a gift from the unfortunate King.

The history of Carisbrooke has not been stirring, but the fortification of the castle was long maintained. Edward I found it sufficiently valuable to negotiate with Isabel de Fortibus for the transfer of it while she lay on her deathbed, and, whether royal or baronial, the possessors of the castle have taken care to preserve it. So its domestic architecture is in every style; it embodies towers and bastions of the Elizabethan period with a keep of the twelfth century. Its most tragic and

CORFE CASTLE.

most famous associations are at the close of its history, for its decline has taken place only in the last two hundred years.

Corfe, in Dorset, a third castle on this short strip of coast, is also a striking reminder of the Civil Wars. Corfe commanded the promontory known as the Isle of Purbeck, but until the Conquest there was no fortification on the spot, for William the Conqueror negotiated for its possession with the Abbess of Shaftesbury. Consequently the Corfe Geat, where, according to the Chronicle, the young King Edward the Martyr was murdered in 987, must be identified with another spot.

The site was ideal for a castle, protected on three sides by the natural steepness of a chalk down, at the base of which two rivers forked on their way to Poole Harbour. The castle was Norman and Edwardian in three wards crowned by a keep. The keep, probably erected by Henry I, was massive, its walls not weakened by interior galleries or chambers; but only one of its walls remains. Its wards were surrounded by admirably constructed curtain walls with projecting round towers, and the gatehouse was protected by drum towers and portcullis; but the towers are now crooked and breached, and the gatehouse is gutted.

Here Baldwin de Redvers held out for Matilda before he retired to the Wight, but its military importance was never great. To many monarchs, to John especially, it was more valuable as a prison. Duke Robert was brought here after Tenchebrai, and Edward II before he was removed to Berkeley Castle. But John starved to death twenty-four French knights at Corfe at one time; his executions were massacres. In one case he put a mother and her son together in one dungeon to die of starvation. The account of their end is one of the most revolting stories in the mediæval chronicles. In another case, a prophet, one Peter de Wakefield, who foretold the end of John's reign, was kept at Corfe to see the outcome of his prophecy. In the predestined year John gave

England in fief to the Pope, and the prophet, who had scored a technical victory undoubtedly, was dragged to death at the heels of wild horses.

Such were the incidents in the history of Corfe. It was a place of great strength, unlikely ever to be tested seriously in local warfare, and it was geographically remote from the strategic centres of the country. By Elizabeth it was granted to Sir Christopher Hatton, and in 1635 it was sold to Sir John Bankes. Its future might have been equally uneventful, and Corfe might have been an admired show-place to-day, but that Dorset suddenly acquired an accidental strategic importance in the Civil Wars. It lay between Oxford and the Royalist stronghold of the South-west. Sherborne and Corfe were the keys to the northern and southern communications with the Cornish peninsula. Twice an inglorious Roundhead army attacked Corfe, which was defended by Lady Bankes. The best accounts of the siege are Royalist, and they tell of the Parliamentarians "filling their men with strong waters even to madnesse," and of their "cowardly leader who had, like Cæsar, been the only man that came sober to the assault, lest he should be valiant against his will." But they did not prevail until one of the garrison turned traitor, and, pretending to introduce newly-recruited defenders, placed all the important posts of the castle in the hands of the enemy.

The House of Commons ordered £10 to be given to the Captain who gave the news of the taking of Corfe, and £10 to the messenger who brought it. Corfe was ordered to be "slighted" or dismantled; an order which was carried out very thoroughly, as we see by the disordered ruins. Heavy charges of gunpowder were used, and also the older device of burning props beneath the undermined towers. The Buttavant Tower has been half blown away, the drum tower of the gatehouse thrown forward, and the encircling walls and bastions thrown down or turned askew.

CASTLE RISING

CASTLE RISING stands in one of the most remote parts of England—in the flat lands of northern Norfolk, two or three miles from the eastern shore of the Wash. Even in our day, although the village of Rising is one of the beauty spots of East Anglia, it is not easy of access; but in the Middle Ages, before drainage and tillage reclaimed so much of the coast lands, the castle must have been inaccessible from all directions except the southern. It is a local tradition that Rising was once a flourishing harbour, and the villagers defy their neighbours of King's Lynn with the old saying that " Rising was a seaport town when Lynn was but a marsh." There are, however, no evidences of former prosperity. The church, a small one of Norman origin, has been tactfully restored in recent times. In the village is the Bede House, founded in 1614 by Henry Howard, Earl of Northampton, for the reception of twelve poor spinsters, with the careful proviso that any one of them found guilty of " atheism, heresy, blasphemy, faction in the hospital, injury, or disgracing the assistants," should be instantly expelled. What a caricature on the enthusiastic Shelley it seems; an impoverished spinster ejected from an almshouse for atheism! But metaphysical questionings and bickerings over dogma have passed them by. They may be seen on Sundays in prim procession to the parish church, clad in red cloaks and black steeple hats of the sixteenth century, for all the world like witches intercepted by the churchwardens. For the rest, it is proof sufficient of Rising's stagnation that it was a pocket borough before the Reform Act.

The earthworks of the castle stand out upon slightly higher ground from the level country surrounding them, and they are

CASTLE RISING

all the more striking because the curtain walls which formerly crowned them have disappeared. An oval, almost round, enclosure formed by high earthen banks has smaller oblong courts flanking its longer sides to east and west. The rectangular shape of the whole has induced some to suppose a Roman origin which cannot be confirmed by archæological or documentary evidence; and the theory presupposes that the Romans found a British oval encampment, which they converted into the rectangular form. More probably the earthworks were built in Anglo-Saxon times, and as in so many other cases utilized, perhaps extended, by the Normans. It is an indication of their size that the oval rampart stands about 30 ft. above the floor of the exterior buildings. The area of the whole is 18 acres.

It is remarkable how completely the buildings have been destroyed. Nothing remains in the flanking courtyards. The approach to the enclosure is by a gap in the east side of the rampart across a ruined bridge and through a Norman gatehouse. The gatehouse, of which two arches and the lower story remain, was of a rectangular type, containing a passage-way 13 feet long between stone walls. Within the enclosure the foundations of some domestic buildings can be traced. They are probably of Tudor date. On the north side is a Norman chapel in a ruinous condition. It consisted of nave, choir, and apse, divided by transverse arches, and it was probably the garrison church. For some time its existence was unknown, until it was found buried in earth which had fallen down from the ramparts. A few short lengths of curtain wall that remain were built in the reign of Henry VII. If there were any Norman walls they have entirely disappeared.

But the most striking object to be seen through the arch of the gatehouse is the Norman keep, which is a compensation for so much that has been destroyed. The keep is low and massive, like those of Norwich and Colchester. In fact, the height is less than either the length or the breadth, and the effect is intensified by the loss of the battlements. Otherwise the exterior is well enough preserved. The side facing the gatehouse is covered by a forebuilding. While the rest of the keep is built of flint rubble with ashlar facings on the pilasters and corner buttresses, the forebuilding is entirely cased in ashlar with many ornamentations, the most striking being a continuous arcade and above it a line of circles containing carved heads, which are to be seen at best advantage on the south side over the entrance archway. This gives entrance to a fine flight of stone stairs leading up to the vestibule tower, which is twice the width of the rest of the forebuilding. The stairs were protected by gates under Norman arches at the bottom, at a landing half-way up, and at the entrance to the vestibule. Below the vestibule, on the basement level of the tower, was a prison entered from above only, and over the vestibule was another floor. Originally the forebuilding had three roofs. The arch on the landing within, and a pilaster buttress without, divided the stairway into two sections of different heights externally, and the vestibule tower was built to the level of the rest of the keep. Within, the stairway was commanded by a *meurtrière* and a loop for archers.

The keep was divided by an interior cross-wall and had only one floor over the basement. The entrance to the basement was by spiral stairs in the north-east and south-west angles of the keep, but there is also a door just inside the entrance archway of the staircase. For many years the basement was filled with rubbish which had dropped from the floor above as the keep fell into ruins. In 1822, when the enclosure was cleared and the Norman chapel discovered, this rubbish was removed. The bases of some columns were found, and a well 63 ft. in depth. The walls are looped for archers.

CASTLE RISING

The vestibule at the top of the stairs contains a beautiful Norman arch, the entrance into the great hall, but at some period this was blocked up and converted into a fireplace. The interior is dilapidated. It possessed living rooms, a hall, chapel, and ante-chapel, and a mural arcade. It seems strange that the keep at Castle Rising should be distinguished among its fellows by the possession of a kitchen and still room. Kitchens are rare in Norman keeps—there is one also at Norwich, not far away—for it was evidently the custom to cook in the buildings outside and bring the dishes to the keep in various degrees of tepidity.

The manor of Snettisham, which embraced the village of Rising, belonged to Archbishop Stigand and was granted at the Conquest to the ubiquitous Odo of Bayeux, Earl of Kent. When Odo rebelled William Rufus gave the manor to William de Albini, the father of the William de Albini who became Lord of Arundel by his marriage with Queen Adela, widow of Henry I. This second William is supposed to have built the keep. He was one of the most chivalrous knights of Europe. He rejected the amorous attentions of the Queen of France because of his love for Adela, and it is said that, when the rejected lady thrust him into a lion's den, William put his hand into the lion's mouth and extracted its tongue. In similar circumstances, during his captivity in Austria, Richard I went even further: he pulled out the lion's heart. In William's case, however, the less drastic operation was sufficient to save his life. The Albini arms bore in commemoration a placid but tongueless lion, and the husband of Adela is known to history as William of the Strong Arm.

In the reign of Edward III Castle Rising belonged to the Crown and was for twenty-seven years the principal dwelling of Isabella " the She-Wolf of France." Although she had betrayed her husband, Edward II, for Mortimer, who was slain by the orders of her son, she had by no means a troubled end, possessing as she did many manors and being treated with unbroken respect. She devoted her considerable energies to the collecting of relics, and falconry, with an occasional pilgrimage to Walsingham, or a sojourn at one of her other manors. Edward III frequently visited her in state at Castle Rising. There is a record that the Borough of King's Lynn sent to " Isabell the old Queen " presents of wine, flesh meats, swans, lampreys, turbot, sturgeon, herrings, and oats for her horses.

She died at Hertford full of years and honour, clothed in the habit of Saint Clare, and was buried in the Franciscan church at Newgate in London. On the tomb of her son, John of Eltham, at Westminster, there is a statue of Isabella, but of the halls and rooms of state at Castle Rising little enough remains.

CASTLE RISING.

THE CHANNEL COAST

THE Kentish promontory is the Achilles' heel of England. There is no other strip of coast that gives to an invader such an immediate advantage over the whole country as that between the North Foreland and Beachy Head. Its possessor has the opportunity to blockade London—the nerve centre of England—by controlling the Thames; he has cut the main communications with the Continent, and he has established his own, if the sea power which transported his army still gives him control of the Narrow Seas.

This was the successful avenue of invasion used by the Romans and by the Normans. Since the Battle of Hastings every large scale attack upon England has been abortive, but the tents of Napoleon's *armée maritime* were to be seen upon the cliffs of Boulogne in the last century, and, only that *Deus afflavit et dissipati sunt*, the captains of the Armada would have attempted to seize the same important part of England.

This history of Kent and Sussex as the cockpit of England is not due to the historical accident that England's invaders have come from Southern Europe and have naturally chosen the shortest sea passage. It is the result of strategic considerations. When the Dauphin of France invaded England on behalf of the Barons of the Charter, he was advised by his father, Philip Augustus, a brilliant strategist, to secure Dover at once and at all costs. But Louis turned to Dover too late and failed before its walls; and Philip, when the news was brought, cried " Then he has not taken one foot of English land."

THE CHANNEL COAST

HASTINGS CASTLE.

Acting with the same considerations, William the Conqueror did not strike directly at London after his crushing victory at Hastings. He marched, instead, along the coast to Dover, secured the hub of the Kentish roads at Canterbury, seized the crossing of the Medway at Rochester, and then advanced along the valley of the Thames for the blockade of London. Nor have England's enemies come invariably from the South. Long before the Romans left the Britons to fend for themselves they had arranged a system of defence—the famous Saxon shore—against the enemy from the north who were to give England her name. The Roman defensive fortresses did not front Jutland and the mouth of the German rivers, but they were arranged along the south-east coast from the Wash to Beachy Head. They were true castles, their walls thick and high, protected by a newly-invented tactical device, the bastion, on account of the increased importance of archery.

Of these Richborough, in Kent, remains an unhappy relic, set on a knoll overlooking flat, marshy fields on every side. It once protected the sea channel that passed behind the Island of Thanet to Reculvers, but it has shared a common fate of Kentish ports in being widowed of the sea. For, owing to the racing of the tides through the Channel's bottle-neck, the coast is blockaded with shifting sands, and one generation has before now seen the complete obstruction of a prosperous harbour.

Richborough Castle is a heap of rubble, stripped of its ashlar covering, and still preserving some of the plan, though none of the appearance, it had in the days of strength. There are interesting contrasts in the neighbourhood of this ruin of Rome. A mile away is Sandwich, a famous port in the Middle Ages. To-day, if one admires the beautiful barbican of chequered stonework, one has seen the sum and total of the military remains of Sandwich. A red-sailed lugger may be observed in the middle of green fields, as it creeps up the winding channel from the sea, and it is difficult to realize that some poor, persistent fishermen still take pride in Sandwich as a port. Then, to crown the contrast, is the modern port of Richborough, the " mystery port " of the war, whence the train ferries set out for France. Already the channel that leads to it through Pegwell Bay is silted up, and the lonely bivouac of concrete huts and rusting ferries is a curious relic of spent energies. Perhaps Richborough will some day become a centre of commerce, but at present it is a fitting epilogue to the story of the Roman fort and the mediæval town.

At Pevensey and Dover, however, are Roman fortresses that added to their military history in later centuries.

Fronting the cliffs of France is a monument to commemorate

the heroes of our generation who formed the Dover Patrol, and at the very heart of the castle is an even older monument with a similar significance. Nearly a score of centuries ago the Roman galleys made the perilous passage from Gessoriacum (Boulogne) to Dubris. At both ports lighthouses were erected to guide the mariners, and the Pharos of Dover still watches over the Channel. An ashlar coating was built around it; the ashlar decayed, but the green sandstone and tufa of the pharos is still sound; it was crowned with Tudor brickwork, and it bears the load. Flanking the lighthouse is a building which may have been a part of the fortifications. Its origin is lost in antiquity. It was certainly a Saxon church; it is the garrison church of St. Mary in Castra to-day, and there is a strong opinion that this building was used as a place of worship by the Christians of Roman times. Probably Dover can boast the oldest Christian

DEAL CASTLE.

church in England. Around it are Roman and Saxon fortifications—the Norman walls and towers, the fine keep of Henry II, with its perfect forebuilding, the great redoubt built after the Dauphin's siege had demonstrated a weakness in the defensive plan.

In all things Dover was England, and Shakespeare made its white cliffs the figure of his country. The names of its constables included Godwin and Earl Harold, Hubert de Burgh, Stephen Langton, the King Maker, Henry VIII, the younger Pitt, and the Duke of Wellington. Matthew Paris spoke of the castle as the " key and lock of the whole realm," and Sir Walter Raleigh wrote " A Discourse of Sea Ports," with the intention mainly of advocating the improvement of Dover. " No promontory, town or haven in Christendom," he wrote, " is so placed by nature and situation both to gratify friends and annoy enemies as Your Majesties town of Dover." In less measure that is true to-day. The guns still point seaward, the bugles call, and the flag flies above the Roman and Norman stones of one of Europe's major fortresses in the twentieth century.

Pevensey (like Porchester, which guarded the great Roman harbour near Portsmouth) is a mediæval castle built within the enclosure of a Roman coast fort. They are symptomatic of the Norman facility for adaptation and of their assumption of the Roman tradition. The walls of Pevensey enclose an area of nine acres wherein lay the settlement of Anderida. The Anglo-Saxon Chronicle makes special note of the destruction of Anderida in the fifth century, and for six hundred years its walls were desolate, until the Conqueror's half-brother, Roger de Mortain, improvised a fortress there which proved to be impregnable. In those days the sea washed its eastern and southern walls, and at high tide flooded the marshy lands which lay around the other sides of the mound on which Pevensey stood. These natural defences were added to in the thirteenth century by an inner curtain wall around the actual castle in the south-east corner, and by an inner moat of some width. The kernel of the completed castle was the mound thrown up by Roger de Mortain surmounted by its strong Norman keep.

William the Conqueror landed at Pevensey, and in the next reign his son Rufus there besieged his uncles Odo of Bayeux and the Earl of Mortain, who had rebelled in favour of his brother, Robert of Normandy; so Pevensey played a great part in the history of that vigorous family. For three months William's direct assaults were unavailing, but he obtained the surrender of the garrison by starvation after an attempt at relief from the Norman fleet had been beaten off. In 1147 Stephen was quite as unsuccessful in his bombardment of Matilda's supporters, but he also compelled the surrender after a strict blockade. In 1264, however, after the battle of Lewes, the tables were turned. Simon de Montfort besieged Pevensey for eight months. He even reached the Roman walls. But the defenders maintained their supplies and communications from the sea until Simon threw up the attempt in despair and marched off to Kenilworth. Pevensey was true to its type: the strength of the castle was relative to the patience, not to the strength, of its besieger.

Under the Tudors the castle was for the first time allowed to fall into decay, and it shared the fate of many a noble building in being used as a quarry by the neighbouring gentry.

Not everyone is aware that the Protector Somerset desired to use the stones of Westminster Abbey for the building of Somerset House. With a like vandalism, which can be more readily excused, the squires set upon Pevensey, and one John Thatcher, may be especially held up for reprobation as the purchaser of six hundred stone loads of Pevensey and English history at the price of twopence a load. It is curiously symbolic that, except for its curtain wall, the mediæval castle is a bewildering ruin, its keep and its hall razed to the ground, while the Roman walls and bastions, robbed of their stone covering, indeed, " still wear their ancient countenance of strength and defiance," to quote an eighteenth-century traveller. It is a strange consideration that after the lapse of so many centuries the Roman remains in England are a more valuable index to their civilization than the archæological survival of the Middle Ages. If no documents survived from either period, we could more surely reconstruct the life of Roman Britain than the times of the Saxons, Normans, or Plantagenets.

The mediæval castle was ultimately as much an evidence of individualism in society as the nineteenth-century factory. The manufacturer has a monopoly of capital, and the castle builder

WALMER CASTLE.

had made a corner in power. The castles were (unlike the mediæval cathedrals) erected against the mob. But when the mob had control there was no need of a castle, and no opportunity for one to be built by an oppressor. The greatest safeguard of the southern coast in the Middle Ages was the fleet of the Cinque Ports, and because the monarchy realized this fact, the towns of that league had their own privileges of jurisdiction and taxation, making them to all intents and purposes a group of collective barons. They had their walls, but not their castles. So it is interesting to find that the monarchy turned its attention to the fortification of the Cinque Ports when it had become supreme over lords and people, an individualist monarchy—the Tudor despotism. A memorandum of Cromwell's, dated 1533, is headed " Articles conceived for the defence of the towns of Dover, Sandwich, Deal, Folston, the Isle Tened (Thanet), and Hythe, and all the sea coasts about."

Dover had always been a royal castle. Fearing invasion from France or Spain, Henry VIII built additional castles and " bulwarks " from Tilbury to Portland, employing as his architect a Moravian, Stephen von Haschenperg. " The Almayn," as men called him, was ingenious enough in the construction of twisting passages and culs-de-sac in which the struggling enemy could be grilled with boiling lead, but castles such as Deal, Sandgate, Walmer, and Camber, were small, and would probably have been of little value if brought to the test of war. Of them all Walmer possesses the most interest as the residence of the Lords Warden of the Cinque Ports. Nelson used to land from his flagship in the Downs to consult with Pitt at Walmer, and the Duke of Wellington, as Warden, lived and died in the castle.

England's safety has long been in her isolation and in her sea power. But we may see in the near future new defensive works

THE CHANNEL COAST

erected on this vulnerable coast. For the aeroplane has narrowed the Narrow Seas and the long-range gun can span them. The modern progress in the art of killing has brought our statesmen face to face with the problem that England has a frontier equally with Germany, Belgium, or France. It may be that the Navy will play a less vital part in the future than it has done in the past. The problem of the south coast has almost become that of safeguarding, not a sea frontier, but a river frontier like the Rhine.

WINCHELSEA CASTLE.

CHEPSTOW

A TOWN with the Saxon name of Chepstow grew up under the shadow of a castle built by the Normans on the Welsh bank of the Wye, and was called by them Ystreigl or Striguil. There was a time when the great merchants of Europe could talk of the lordship of Striguil as a great centre of commerce. It held one of the gates to Wales; it contained a large part of the Wye valley, and the Wye valley boasted Tintern, an abbey under the patronage of the successive lords of Striguil, where the wool trade was carefully fostered by the monks.

A book of history might not tell us more. First, the purely military outpost of the Normans is set up in 1067 as a bridgehead for further advances into Wales. The Norman scribe, true to the racial instinct for adaptation, copies down the barbarous Welsh name of the locality as it strikes his ear. Then the merchants come, and the English town of Chepstow (which means literally a place of trade, a market) grows great under the protection of the feudal magnates, outlives them, and finally extends its own name to the ruined walls of Striguil. It is the emergence of England, made possible by an infusion of Norman strength. The powerless dragon of Wessex goes down in defeat at Hastings, and a few centuries later the battle cry of Agincourt is " St. George for Merry England." The point illustrated at Chepstow could be easily proved : that the battle of Hastings was the decisive blow for the English conquest of England; it was the final defeat of the Northmen.

The name of Striguil is probably derived from a Welsh verb meaning to wander, in reference to the winding course of the river. But a most interesting theory was once built up to show

CHEPSTOW

that the origin of the name lay in the Welsh *Ystrad Iwl*; that Chepstow was a Roman station to protect the river-crossing of the Strata Julia. Unfortunately there was never a Roman station at Chepstow, the Strata Julia was in another part of the country, and the Roman road to Caerleon and Caerwent passed over the Wye some little way up stream. The first military use of the site was undoubtedly made by William Fitz Osborn, Seneschal of Normandy, Earl of Hereford, who was made joint Justiciar of the kingdom with Odo of Bayeux, with instructions to build castles in suitable positions while William the Conqueror was visiting Normandy in 1067.

Chepstow (as the castle will be called to avoid confusion) was built upon an ideal river-side position which it would have been folly to neglect. The old bridge of the Roman road was near enough to be afforded military protection, and as the town grew up a new bridge was thrown across the Wye a little below the castle. The castle was built upon a long and narrow platform along the Wye. On one side sheer limestone cliffs rose from the waters of the river, and on the other side was a steep gully or ravine running parallel to the stream. The town, a walled enclosure, grew up by the side of the ravine, affording additional protection, if it was needed, from that direction. The walls of the town are fairly well preserved, and Chepstow is a rare example of a castle associated with the fortifications of a town but lying entirely outside the town walls; a disposition partly due to the nature of the site and partly to the fact that the castle was the original settlement. The platform of rock, some 250 yards in length, and in breadth varying from 30 to 70 yards, rises towards the centre where the original Norman castle was erected.

Chepstow is long and narrow, consisting of four adjacent wards, occupying the whole length of the tongue of land. On such a site the concentric form was impossible, but attack was only to be feared from east and west. The original castle probably took the form of a ward near the western end of the platform. A deep ditch was excavated from the ravine to the cliff on the west to protect an elongated enclosure with a massive and defensible hall at its eastern end. Probably there were also domestic quarters in wood, which have disappeared. The first addition, in the twelfth century, was a large ward to the east of this, and in the next hundred years a barbican was built at the western end of the castle, and the strongest ward of all, with living quarters, gatehouse, and a strong tower, was added in the east.

The strength of the castle is at once obvious to the visitor. The barbican, not a narrow passage but an enclosed courtyard, is fronted by a ditch, crossed by a drawbridge. Within the barbican, against the wall of the second court, is the old ditch of the Norman castle. The entrance of the barbican is protected by an imposing gatehouse with rectangular towers in two stories and the usual apparatus of gate and portcullis, battlement and loop. At the south-west angle is a round tower which was formerly connected with the enceinte of the town by a wall across the ravine of no great strength. Having taken the well-protected barbican by assault an enemy would find himself confronted by the ditch and drawbridge protecting the second cross wall.

The most imposing feature of the whole castle, and indeed one of the most remarkable buildings in any English castle, is the hall or keep at the end of this second ward from the western end. It is of the same class as the fine hall at Richmond, of early Norman work with twelfth and thirteenth century additions. Probably (and here as usual the experts differ) it was built immediately after the Conquest, to judge by the style of architecture, and the irregularities of its plan and construction. The ordinary visitor may leave on one side the alternative and equally attractive theories that a hall was converted into a keep and that a keep was converted into a hall. It may be considered a hall capable of defence like the similar buildings at Richmond and Durham.

The building occupies the end of the ward, leaving a narrow gallery on the side of the river, closed by gates at either end, to connect the second and third wards. The basement of the building was used for stores, and its walls are pierced with loops to command the gallery. The Norman *aula* in the upper story is now entered by a vice in the thickness of the wall. The fireplace must have been in the centre of the floor with an opening in the roof to allow of the escape of smoke. The hall shows its continued use, for the ornamentation is mostly Decorated. Norman windows have been blocked out and windows of the thirteenth century inserted in their stead, and a line of Decorated windows takes the place of a triforium in the Norman hall. At one end an arch has been built up dividing the hall into two unequal parts. This provided a solar for the lord and his friends, and the line of Decorated windows above the string course provided light for a broad wooden gallery running around the hall.

The third ward from the west has no outstanding features, except a watch tower in the southern curtain projecting towards the ravine. From the top of this tower signals could formerly be received from a similar tower on a high hill across the river. By this means ships entering the mouth of the Wye could be seen long before they reached Chepstow, where the lord had the right to exact toll from them. The other tower still stands on Twt Hill —which means look-out hill. There is a Twt Hill above Carnarvon, and the name remains in some English villages, such as Toot Baldon in Oxfordshire.

In the fourth or lower ward the thirteenth-century builders erected their most elaborate buildings and their strongest fortifications. The buildings have been allowed to fall into disrepair, and we can only see from their range and variety, from an occasional room or window, that they must once have been of considerable magnificence. They included a hall, an oratory, kitchens, and dwelling rooms, running along the cliff top over the Wye. The most interesting of the surviving portions is the vaulted cellar with a groined roof excavated below the hall. A door in the floor opens above a creek or recess in the cliff, and an iron ring shows that use was made of this unusual postern to draw up provisions, messages, and spies. The Royalists besieged in this castle are recorded to have let a boat down to the river in preparation for escape; but a Roundhead soldier swam across the Wye with a knife in his mouth, cut the rope, and brought away the boat.

The landward walls of this court are of immense thickness, even for their period. They are built up of an outer and an inner wall, with a filling of earth between, making a thickness of 20 ft. in places.

The splendid gatehouse is in the north-east angle of the ward near the river. Two drum towers of unequal size defended a gateway with two portcullises, and a projecting archway above commanded the space before the gate. Then, to protect the angle of the ward a strong tower of great strength was built, comparable with the Eagle tower at Carnarvon. It flanked the gatehouse on its left, and the ravine along the line of the south curtain, and to increase its flanking properties stone spurs were built up along its base in the form of demi-pyramids dying away in the face of the tower. Its name is the Marten's tower—so-called because Henry Marten, one of the regicides, having been spared the death penalty, was condemned to an easy imprisonment there after the Restoration.

The entrance to Marten's tower is from the ground level in the ward, protected by its own gate and portcullis. Besides an underground chamber there are three floors, containing one room each, connected by a spiral staircase in the wall. Where the rampart wall communicates with the tower there is another door and portcullis. Jutting from the tower and rising above the level of the ramparts there is a square projection containing a small oratory. Marten's tower was primarily a flanking tower, but it also served as the nearest approach to a keep that was ever attained in the concentric type of castle.

Chepstow belonged to men who made their name in England, Wales, and Ireland. It soon passed out of the hands of the FitzOsborns. William was killed in Flanders, and his son, Roger of Breteuil, was deprived of his estates for conspiracy. The castle was granted to the founder of Tintern Abbey, Walter FitzRichard, of the family of Clare, and thence it descended to Gilbert and Richard Strongbow, the powerful Earls of Pembroke.

For a time Thomas de Brotherton, a son of Edward I, held the castle, regranting it for life to the younger Despenser. To this period may be assigned the reconstruction of the hall, and parts of the lower ward. Subsequently the castle passed through the hands of Mowbrays, Herberts, and Somersets. The Dukes of Beaufort are the present owners.

In the Civil Wars Chepstow was taken by assault, after a cannonade, by the Parliamentarians. A breach was made in the walls, and some forty of the garrison were slain, but it does not appear that very considerable damage was done to the old walls of the castle, which will last for many years to come.

CHILLINGHAM

CHILLINGHAM CASTLE is an interesting and beautiful example of what was rather a fortified manor house than a castle. It was small in extent, lacking any complex defensive system, and accordingly it was easily adapted at a later period to express the newer beauties of the Renaissance. Nevertheless, Chillingham was of significance in Northumbria for its connection with the great families and their feuds, while it was by no means unimportant as a defence against the Scots.

In Northumberland every place of any pretensions was necessarily built so that it could be defended at need. The kings of England were constantly issuing licences to crenellate, that is, to erect battlements; and especially after David's destructive invasion, which ended at Neville's Cross in 1346, the Crown undoubtedly ceased to regard private fortifications on the border with suspicion, and did everything in its power to encourage their erection. Consequently the Border was dotted with pele towers, bastle houses, and other isolated defences, in addition to the castles-in-chief, such as Norham and Warkworth, which were extensive and strong. An example of a bastle house (so called from the French *bastille*) is to be found in Chillingham Park. Hebburn Bastle is a compact gabled dwelling-house, strongly built, and significantly devoid of windows near the ground, with walls of great thickness. The estate in which it stood was added to Chillingham Park in the eighteenth century. Houses of this kind—provided with dungeons as well as with living-rooms—must once have been very common on the Border.

CHILLINGHAM CASTLE.

It was in 1344 that Edward III, " of his special favour," conceded the privilege and gave licence to his beloved and faithful Thomas de Heton to erect around his manor house of Chevelyngham a wall of lime or stone, to crenellate it, and to make it into a castle or fortalice. Four years later the work must have been finished, for in a document (which gravely states also that Julius Cæsar founded and endowed the parish church of Chillingham) the lord of the manor gave to the Vicar of Chillingham a chamber over the gate of his castle, and the right to stable two horses.

There is a curious sidelight upon a day in the life of a borderer afforded by the *Proof of Age* of Margaret Heton in the fourteenth century. To settle a date in dispute it was the sensible custom of the Middle Ages to tap the flow of local tradition; just as in the last century the Irish dated all things by the Year of the Great Wind. Margaret Heton was born in Chillingham Castle on January 14, 1395, and of this there could be no question, for on the day of her baptism by a canon of Alnwick Abbey, Nicholas Heron was married in the church; John Serjeant was wedded to Alice Wyndegaltes; Sir William Heton bought a white horse from William Cramlington, and sent Wyland Mauduit to Newcastle to buy wine; John Belsise rode to Alnwick with a letter to the Earl of Northumberland; William Cotys slew a doe in the field of Chillingham; and John Horsley, carried off a prisoner by the Scots, was avenged by John Wytton, who brought Thomas Turnbull, a Scot, to the dungeons of Chillingham. On the same day Sir Thomas Gray of Heton kidnapped one Thomas Horne, and lodged him a prisoner in Norham, so that Margaret's age was fixed irrevocably.

The family of de Heton died out at Chillingham at the beginning of the fifteenth century, and from 1443 the Grays of Wark possessed the castle. A Sir John de Gray was granted by Henry V the county of Tanquerville on the north bank of the Seine, near Havre, as a reward for his services, in 1419. The gift was held on the terms of homage and the annual delivery of a bassinet (or helmet) at the castle of Rouen on the Feast of St. George. A strange service, symbolical, and not arduous. A more deserving feudatory was the man of Kent, who enjoyed his manor on condition that he held the king's head whenever he crossed the Channel; but this idle tale may be founded upon a misreading of the word " bassinet." Both Tanquerville and Rouen were lost to the English, so the stipulated service was soon impossible to perform, but the owners of Chillingham to this day are the Earls of Tankerville.

CHILLINGHAM

Sir Ralph Gray, the brave defender of Bamburgh, who was executed at Doncaster in 1464, was foresighted enough to convey Chillingham in trust to the vicar of Wooler and Edmund Burrell before falling foul of Edward IV; and, in consequence, his widow, Jacquetta, was in possession at her death in 1469. During the Pilgrimage of Grace, Chillingham was held for Henry VIII, and it is recorded that Sir Ingram Percy, who had " a willing, malicious stomach " against the King, sent to Berwick for great ordnance to besiege it.

Of the castle as it stands to-day it can be said that the four corner towers date originally from the time of Sir Thomas de Heton in the middle of the fourteenth century. But the connecting buildings which form a courtyard are of much later date, even later than 1541, when the castle was " newly reparelled " by Sir Robert Ellerker during the minority of Ralph Gray.

The most noticeable feature within the courtyard is the façade on the east side, attributed to Inigo Jones, with the graceful stair in the centre, leading to the dining-hall. The niches in the façade contain the weather-worn figures of seven of the Nine Worthies in classic garb. The Nine Worthies were: Joshua, David, and Judas Maccabeus; Hector, Alexander, and Julius Cæsar; Arthur, Charlemagne, and Godfrey of Bouillon. The ordinary person would be loth to discriminate against any two of such an exemplary company, and there is a certain interest in speculating as to the sculptor's surely reluctant omissions. But beyond a hazardous list of probabilities it is impossible to tell the tale of the Seven Worthiest.

Chillingham is famous for its herd of wild white cattle which roam about the picturesque park. The Chillingham cattle form one of the few herds surviving from the more spacious days when England was not yet honeycombed with hedge and dyke.

CHILLINGHAM

Their strain is pure, and they have a long history at Chillingham Castle, a history which probably began when the park was enclosed during the reign of Henry III. At that time wild cattle

CHILLINGHAM CASTLE.

were to be found in many parts of England (in the Chilterns chiefly, and in Epping Forest) and in Scotland. Now the interesting survivals are carefully bred according to the most orthodox Mendelian principles, but as the cattle themselves are ignorant of the solicitude with which their immaculate white coats and long horns tipped with black are preserved from plebeian mutations, they still fancy themselves wild, run away at the approach of a stranger, and refuse to touch any object which smells of man. There are some interesting old prints of the Chillingham cattle, showing the constitutional incapacity of our forefathers to draw a cow (nor could they draw a horse, as old racing pictures testify), but Landseer, in the last century, observed more carefully, and left a more faithful record of the Chillingham breed.

CHIRK

MRS. THRALE and Dr. Johnson visited Chirk in Denbighshire during their tour in Wales. Mrs. Thrale commented in her diary: " Chirk Castle is by far the most enviable dwelling I have yet ever seen, ancient and spacious, full of splendour and dignity, yet with every possible convenience of obscurity and retirement. Here we saw the best Library we have been shown in Wales, and a ridiculous Chaplain, whose conversation with Mr. Johnson made me ready to burst with laughing. . . ." Johnson himself in his diary made only a formal reference to the castle (and no reference at all to the Chaplain), but he wrote home to Boswell " that one of the castles in Wales would contain all the castles that he had seen in Scotland."

Chirk, in its day a strong Marcher stronghold, is not well known, but it is said to be one of the largest inhabited houses in Britain, and its area was greater formerly than now. The castle stands upon a slight eminence above the valley of the Ceiriog (a tributary of the Dee) overlooking thirteen counties, with the command of a gap in the famous Offa's Dyke. The present castle cannot be anything but an Edwardian foundation, much restored and altered, but its position was of earlier importance. In the village of Chirk is the mound of a Norman fortress, and the place is to be identified with a battlefield where Henry II was resisted in an expedition into Wales.

Powel, the Elizabethan historian of Wales, describes the forcing of Offa's Dyke, where " there was, and is at this daie, a

CHIRK

narrow way through the same ditch (for that ditch appeareth yet to this daie verie deep through all that countrie and beareth his old name) these men, I say, as they would have passed the straite, were met withall, and greate number of them slaine, as appeareth by their graves, there yet to be seen, whereof the name, Adw'r Beddau, or Pass of the Graves."

The Edwardian castle was erected at the end of the thirteenth century by Roger Mortimer, to whom the lordship of Chirk was granted on account of the forfeiture of " Llewelini Vaughan, inimici Regis." It was simple in plan, of some strength, and noticeably of a type transitional between the castle and the fortified manor house, because there are no traces of outworks or subsidiary defences, nor was the slope on which it stood sufficient to preclude assault from any quarter. On the other hand, the builders of Chirk did not neglect its defences. It was a square building, the sides defended midway by round towers of half projection, and the angles by similar towers of three-quarter projection. This formed a courtyard around which were the domestic buildings. An elaborate main gatehouse was probably on the south side, opposite to the simple gateway which now serves as an entrance. Such a compact castle must have been reputed strong and easily defended. The towers (or more properly, bastions) were massive, their ramparts level with the curtain, and their walls looped for archers. There were probably no windows in the curtain, for those in the domestic buildings looked into the court, and the outside windows now to be seen are all square Tudor openings.

The castle has been often restored, but the western midtower (known as Adam's Tower) and the curtain meeting it are practically untouched. In Adam's Tower the window embrasures are 16 feet in depth, and the rock on which it stands has been hollowed out into a dungeon which receives light and air only from a chute connecting with the quadrangle. The gateway, between the mid-tower and the eastern flanking tower on the north side, is curiously simple, consisting of a pointed arch placed within a tall sustaining arch which rises nearly the whole height of the curtain.

CHIRK CASTLE

The gatehouse was so much a part of the Edwardian type of castle that we may presume it existed once in the southern side, of which not a trace remains, for the restoration of various centuries have altered the original plan of Chirk. The southern wall without any flanking towers runs only just south of the demi-towers that were originally at the centre of the eastern and western sides. There is no record to show when this change took place. The chapel which occupies the south-eastern angle of the castle has fifteenth-century windows, and the rest of the present south side was obviously used for a hall and kitchens, but as this portion was certainly rebuilt in the seventeenth century, it is impossible to say why or when the plan of Chirk was so strangely transformed.

The lordship of Chirk commanded the Dee and Ceiriog route into Wales, and the Roger Mortimer who held it was one to make use of his opportunities. In 1308 to " Roger Mortuo Mari of Chirk " Edward II committed the custody of all Wales, with the castle of Carnarvon and the office of Justice, and from that time to his death he was said to " rule Wales like a King." But his pride was short-lived, for he rashly took arms against the favourite Despensers, with the result that he lost Chirk, which was sold to the Earl of Arundel.

In the fifteenth century Chirk had many owners, but its military history is obscure, though it obviously suffered in Owen Glendower's rebellion, for the Earl of Arundel marched into Wales and fought Glendower's ally, Hotspur, near Cadr Idris, and in 1405, the Chirk estates being devastated, Arundel was forced to borrow from the king to cover the expenses of his marriage.

In 1423 Chirk was again at royal disposal. It was granted to John de Radeclyf, Knight, in consideration of the fact that the King owed him £7,029 13s. 1d. over and above his wages of 4s. a day as seneschal of Aquitaine and other items duly paid. But the most engaging of these owners of Chirk was Sir William Stanley, a humble understudy to the King-Maker. Stanley was Chamberlain of Chester under Edward IV, and created Justiciar of North Wales by Richard III, but his respect for his dread sovereign lord is shown by a letter explaining his absence from

CHIRK

a hunting party: "beying so besy with olde Dyk," he says, "I can have no layf thereunto." He showed his solicitude for "olde Dyk" in another fashion at Bosworth, when he led the men of Chirk among his supporters, for he decided the battle by changing sides, and then, picking the crown out of a bush, loyally placed it on the head of Henry Tudor. History does not say who placed it in the bush, but quite possibly it was Sir William Stanley.

As Lord Chamberlain he was now one of the most important subjects in the kingdom, and reputed to be the richest. He repaired Chirk, which probably suffered heavily in the wars. Leland wrote: "At Chirk self be a few houses, and there is on a small hille a mighty large and stronge castel with divers towers late well repayred by Sir William Standeley, the Yerle of Derby's brother." This rather discounts an Elizabethan report that Chirk was "rased to the ground, saving one tower, here commonly called Adam's Tower," but the writer was probably of a morbid turn of mind, because he went on to say that in Chirk township there were "twenty-four burgesses in decay."

Sir William Stanley found his match in Henry Tudor, who soon disposed of his too powerful friend. As Camden tersely put the matter, in an account of the various owners of Chirk: "And afterwards to Sir William Stanley, Chamberlaine to King Henry VII, who, contesting with his soveraigne about his good services (when he was honorably recompensed) lost his head, forgetting that soveraigne must not be beholding to subjects."

After that Chirk passed to Elizabeth's Dudley, and ultimately to Sir Thomas Middleton, one time Lord Mayor of London, who settled the estate upon his son. As befitted a London man, the latter took the side of Parliament in the Civil Wars, when

CHIRK

Chirk was twice besieged. Sir Thomas Middleton the younger was a dangerous enemy to the Crown, for he was in a position to influence his countrymen, and in 1643 he was created by Parliament Sergeant-Major-General of the six northern counties of Wales. Accordingly the Shropshire Royalists were ordered to seize Chirk, which they were able to do, so that in 1644 Middleton found himself not the besieged, but the besieger of his own castle. A letter from the governor, Sir John Watts, to Prince Rupert, gives some account of the action from the Royalist point of view.

" May it please your Highness,—This gentleman journeying towards Oxford, I most humbly beseech leave to present to your Highness by him an account of a late action of the rebels. They attempted to work into the castle with iron crows and pickers under great planks and tables which they had erected against the castle side for their shelter, but my stones beat them off. They acknowledged in Oswestry they had 31 slain by the castle and 43 others hurt; their prime engineer was slain by the castle-side; they are very sad for him. If your Highness please, this gentleman will very fully impart all the passages during the siege to your Highness; he was in the castle with me. I shall not presume to be further tedious. I most humbly kiss your Highness' sweet hands, and will ever be Your Highness' most humble and assuredly faithful servant, JOHN WATTS."

The absence of mention of artillery in this account is explained in the " Mercurius Aulicus," a Royalist newspaper: " He would not abuse the castle with ordnance (because it was his own house), but fell on with fire-locks at a sink-hole, where the Governor, Col. Watts, was ready to receive him; and gave a pretty number admittance (having an inner work within that hole), but when he saw his opportunity he knocked them all down that came in. . . ."

CHIRK

In 1645 King Charles, marching north to join Montrose, stopped at Chirk, and again on his hurried retreat southward from Chester. But the tide had turned against the monarch, and in 1646, despite his protestations of fidelity, and although Chirk was unmolested at the time, Sir John Watts was negotiating with Parliament for a voluntary surrender. He was offered (and accepted) his freedom, with the sum of £200. Sir Thomas Middleton came into his own, but not by his military prowess.

However, he soon began to tire of the Roundheads. After the death of Cromwell he was found among the gentlemen of the Cheshire Rising, and besieged at Chirk by General Lambert " with a good body of horse and foot and a train of artillery " to which the Council of State added " a mortar piece with shells for the reducement of Chirke Castle."

In a short time Lambert secured the surrender of Chirk. The persons of the garrison were spared, but Lambert was instructed by Parliament " to see that Chirke Castle be demolished and made untenable." And it is said that one side of the castle was actually so demolished.

Chirk Castle is now the dwelling of Lord Howard de Walden, who has done much for its restoration. But the building itself remains a historical problem. The north and east sides have been much rebuilt, the south side has been most probably entirely rebuilt, and it is difficult to date any of the operations. There are records of restoration in 1636, yet there is no sign of damage done during the Civil War, and there is no trace of destruction deliberately carried out by Parliament. Possibly the south side was destroyed by Stanley, and the projected works of 1636 were postponed until the Restoration. Among the treasures of that period at Chirk is a cabinet, the decorations of which are said to have been painted by Rubens. It was

CHIRK

presented by Charles II to the Middleton family in acknowledgment of their belated services.

The position of Chirk, once of great military strength, is still very beautiful, and in the present day we can sympathize with the rhapsodies of the Elizabethan traveller poet, Thomas Churchyard:

> I entered first at Chirke, right ore a brooke,
> Where staying still, on countrey well to looke,
> A Castle fayre appeerde to sight of eye
> Whose walles were gret and towers both large and hye.

DURHAM

ROBERT HEGGE, a Durham man, and Fellow of Corpus Christi College, Oxford, who wrote "The Legend of St. Cuthbert" in the time of James I, invented the most clever gibes that have been directed against the legends of St. Cuthbert, and the most beautiful phrases that have been used to describe Durham. Speaking of the promontory, where the congregation of St. Cuthbert finally settled with the body of their saint, he says: "The topographie of Dunholme at that tyme was, that it was more beholding to Nature for Fortification than Fertilitie: where thick Woods both hindred the Starres from viewing the Earth, and the Earth from the prospect of Heaven." But the trees were cut down, and upon a plateau protected on three sides by a horseshoe bend in the River Wear grew up the cathedral, the castle, and between them, the original town of Durham.

Writing a little sadly perhaps of his own day, Hegge remarks: "he that hath seene the situation of this Citty, hath seene the Map of Sion, and may save a journey to Jerusalem. She is girded almost around with the renowned River of Weer in which, as in a Glasse of Crystall, shee might once have beheld the beauty but now the ruine of her Walls." Durham, with her double crown of cathedral and castle was described by Scott as "half church of God, half castle 'gainst the Scot," and Hegge, speaking in a more practical idiom of the subterranean galleries supposed to connect the cathedral with the citadel, expressed the same idea: "by those caverns it is certain, that the abbey and the castle shake hands under ground."

DURHAM

That was, possibly, a confused simile, but Durham's historical origins made it necessary that the religious and the military elements should shake hands. Primarily the place was a refuge from marauding pagans, and no doubt a town grew up as soon as the neck of the promontory was fortified with a stockade. At least twice before the Conquest—in 1018 and again in 1038—the citizens successfully beat off the kings and the hosts of Scotland. After Hastings they only submitted to William when Sweyn of Denmark failed to send the assistance he had promised; but soon after their submission the people of Durham set upon Robert Cumin whom the Conqueror had made Earl of Northumberland. The Earl was murdered, seven hundred of his soldiers were massacred, and a large part of the city including, it is thought, the Bishop's palace, was burnt to the ground. Then William laid waste the North, and in 1072, returning from an expedition against Malcolm of Scotland, he ordered a castle to be built at Durham.

Thereafter the histories of monastery and castle were more closely linked together. Durham became even more obviously a place where the lion lay down with the lamb, for the bishopric was erected into a palatinate, and the palatine bishop had temporal as well as spiritual jurisdiction, with his own mint, his own courts, and every power that did not override his homage to the sovereign. He was " rex atque sacerdos," the ruler of a district which was supposed to be a buffer state between England and Scotland. His position was expressed on many of the episcopal seals : the obverse represented a bishop, seated, in the act of blessing, and the reverse depicted a mounted warrior with drawn sword, wearing a mitre encircled by a crown.

The episcopal power was also shown in Durham Castle, where princely magnificence was not overshadowed by military necessity. Neither the Tower of London nor Richmond combined to a greater degree pomp with power. By 1075 the castle was already defensible, for, on the approach of Danish raiders, the Archbishop of York warned Bishop Walcher of Durham to provide his stronghold with necessities for a siege. And when, a few years later, Walcher was murdered by a mob, the castle successfully sustained a four days' siege by his murderers. His successor, William de St. Carileph, in rebellion against William Rufus, defied his sovereign's threats in the riverside fastness. Then Ralph Flambard was appointed to the bishopric, but, although a great builder, his only work at Durham was to restore the walls and to build the wall between the choir of the cathedral and the keep.

Quite the most extraordinary of Durham's rulers was William Cumin, a clerk in the episcopal household, who intruded himself into the see on the death of Galfrid Rufus in 1140. During four years neither anathema nor siegecraft could dislodge him, assisted as he was by an unscrupulous character and political advantages. David of Scotland and Matilda were on his side, the majority of the chapter which might elect a bishop canonically were in his custody and all the palatine barons, except one, supported his usurpation. In addition, he procured a Cistercian monk of his own kidney who solemnly arrived with forged letters of congratulation from the Pope. Then Cumin sent his emissary to Scotland, where David was duly impressed by the documents, but an astute and sceptical Abbot of Melrose Abbey exposed the fraud. At length William de St. Barbara was elected at York, Henry II lending him aid for the recovery of his see, and when a concourse of barons and bishops appeared before Durham, Cumin suddenly capitulated. A shivering penitent, he craved absolution before William de St. Barbara and the Archbishop of York, and was thenceforward hidden from historians in a penitential obscurity.

DURHAM

During the episcopate of Bishop Pudsey (1153–95) one of the disastrous fires not uncommon in mediæval times occurred at Durham, so that much of the Norman work at the castle must be ascribed to him. In fact, Durham possesses some of the finest examples of later Romanesque work in England. As a whole, however, the castle is a not altogether unpleasing medley of architectural effects. A succession of bishops felt it their peculiar glory to add a hall, a gallery, or a chapel, to insert a doorway, or to buttress a wall. During the Middle Ages rich and powerful prelates such as Bek, Hatfield, Langley, Fox, and Tunstall, whose names had far more than a local significance, were not unwilling, when they added some new glory, to obscure thereby the equally beautiful work of their predecessors. But during the Commonwealth the English castles suffered from the mutilation and desecration which had befallen the English churches a century before. What the good Hegge says of " abbys " may, in this connection, be applied also to castles. " But Time that hath the sublunary world for her continuall banquette, hath so fed upon these ancient buildings, that some shee hath quite devoured, others pickt to the bones; and what she left for standing dishes, hostilitie hath quite eaten up and defaced." The Commonwealth, in 1649, sold Durham Castle to Thomas Andrewes, Lord Mayor of London, for £1,267 0s. 10d., and by him it was much defaced. Cosin, the first bishop after the Restoration, declared also that the castle was spoiled and ruined by the Scots with gunpowder.

Bishop Cosin spent large sums and exercised considerable taste in restoration, but he was the last man to whom any considerable gratitude is due in that connection. The work of Barrington, in the nineteenth century, was not uniformly fortunate, and in 1833 the castle was given over to the use of Durham University. A better use for a fortress which serves no present military purpose could not be devised, but the inevitable results have been to the detriment of the buildings from an architectural viewpoint, a noticeable misfortune being the subdivision of a Norman hall into smaller rooms and corridors.

The castle as Pudsey left it was a magnificent example of Norman fortification. An artificial mound surmounted by an octagonal keep overlooked the courtyard which ran westward to the cliffs 100 feet above the River Wear. The gateway was on the southern side where the plateau upon which cathedral and castle stood gave the only easy access. The inner archways of the gateway alone show its Norman origin. It was restored by Tunstall, and unhappily modernized by Barrington a century ago, " according to the improved taste of the age," to quote the usual phrase behind which our forefathers have so often sheltered themselves. The keep has had a similar history, but it makes no pretence to be ancient; for the original citadel was rebuilt by Hatfield in the fourteenth century, and again having suffered from decay was re-erected along the lines of the mediæval foundations in 1849 for the incongruous purpose of housing undergraduates.

Pudsey was also primarily responsible for the range of buildings in three stories along the north curtain. As at Richmond the basement, under the hall, was used for storage, so as to preserve the open space of the enclosure for the muster of the garrison. But at the eastern end of the range is a chapel, or rather the undercroft of a chapel, which is early Norman in character and must be aboriginal. It is badly lighted by modern windows, but it possesses more than a little interest for its rough herring-bone pavement and the varied sculptures on the capitals of its slender columns. But the glory of the Norman castle must surely have been the great doorway giving access to the hall on the first floor. This has been little restored, and the arch is a deep mass of pattern carving in four orders. Unfortunately Tunstall concealed the Norman face of the building with a corridor which, despite an oriel window opposite, darkens the doorway, but on the other hand may have preserved its details from decay.

Through the archway was the great hall, and above it on the second floor, approached by a spiral stairway, was another, once known as the Constable's Hall, and to-day, as the Norman Gallery.

In the Constable's Hall the walls were constructed in a continuous arcade with windows in every other archway, detached shafts in couples being between the windows. The full effect of this can hardly be appreciated to-day. It is noticeable, nevertheless, how much care was lavished upon the refinements of domestic architecture, though not at the expense of the provisions for defence. At that time kings were not so nobly housed. Along the shorter western curtain Bek, at the end of the thirteenth century, raised a great hall on an earlier foundation. This is now used as the dining hall of University College, which thereby possesses a hall no less beautiful than those of many of the Oxford Colleges. It is typical of Durham that Bek's range (very much rebuilt by his successors) has a most beautiful exterior not marred by buttresses added at a later period, and a porch erected by Cosin at the Restoration. Cosin also built the fine staircase within.

At Worcester, Rochester, Hereford, and Lincoln, castle and cathedral were also grouped together, but none of these had sites comparable in strength or beauty with that of Durham, and none of these were ruled by bishops with such powers as the palatines of Durham. These built their cathedral to the glory of the heavenly ruler, and the castle to the glory of the earthly ruler. They sat secure upon their eminence, ready to offer to good men a sanctuary and to wicked men a very stout resistance.

KENILWORTH

WARWICKSHIRE is a county of pleasant names and of many legends. The extent of the Forest of Arden lessened, in some degree, the influence of Roman or Saxon in the district, and retained for many of its villages and parks the Celtic names that strike so pleasantly upon the ear. Its romantic associations are no less intriguing than their setting. At Coventry is the home of the Godiva legend, at Warwick the saga of Sir Guy, at Kenilworth the Amy Robsart story, and at Stratford-on-Avon—may one say?—the legend of William Shakespeare.

At least, one may in such a fashion protest that the ample and prosperous acres of Warwickshire have been etherealized by the lovers of romance. From countries where Shakespeare gives precedence to Byron and Scott, pilgrims come to gaze at the ruins of Kenilworth, which Scott invested with glory in his inaccurate account of the tragedy of Amy Robsart. From America come equally enthusiastic Shakespeare lovers to Stratford-on-Avon; to the cottage of Anne Hathaway, which Shakespeare deserted for so long; and to Chalcote Park, where he hung up a lampoon. The true lover of Shakespeare will see Stratford, certainly, but he will seek the poet in all English countryside, in Southwark, and on the Thames Embankment, where Francis Thompson held horses' heads.

Alas! that Godiva's penance is a fiction! And Kenilworth's ivy-mantled ruins bear nobler memories than that of the despicable Robert Dudley, or of his wife who died—by accident for all we know—in Oxfordshire. Nevertheless, it is for these more superficial associations that the romantic come to Kenilworth,

KENILWORTH

and, in their dream-wrapt innocence, they desecrate the beautiful lanes of Warwickshire with char-à-banc and motor-bus.

"Kenilworth" the novel permanently changed the character of Kenilworth the castle, in the minds of men. The visitor brings with him his own impression of the graceful palace where the Earl of Leicester entertained the Renaissance court of Elizabeth with masques and pageantry. He is blind to the massive fortress in which the younger Simon de Montfort held out against Henry III after Evesham. Kenilworth is one of those castles in which the domestic element came gradually to overshadow the military aspect, but its history (except for those seventeen days of courtiers' revels) was a stern one of civil war, and the ruins of Dudley's flimsy additions should symbolize for the visitor their relative position, architecturally and historically.

Both Kenilworth and Warwick were Norman castles, members of the great Midland group, and in both cases the builders showed a keen sense of local geography. Kenilworth was erected at the beginning of the twelfth century upon a knoll of sandstone and gravel in the midst of low-lying ground intersected by many small tributaries of the Avon.

These conditions were turned fully to account as the science of castle building progressed, and the evolution of the fortress illustrates an interesting tendency for the castle itself to lose its earlier character of passive strength, and to take an active part in its own defence, by forcing the enemy to attack on a small number of carefully defended points.

The earliest buildings occupied the site of what was later the Inner Ward upon the mound, and they had, as their citadel, the rectangular keep, called Julius Cæsar's Tower, built without the usual interior cross wall, but with massive square turrets at the four corners, and a fore-building to protect its entrance. These fore-buildings marked the principle just alluded to in its earlier stages. In the first keeps the defenders entered the door high in the wall by a ladder, drew up the ladder, and defied the enemy swarming around the unbroken base wall.

The fore-building gave a permanent approach to the door of the keep by means of a covered stair, defended by an outer door on the ground level, by wrong turnings often enough, by *meurtrières* through which the attackers shepherded together on the stair could be assailed at close range, and by a strong, easily defended door in the keep wall. The main principle still was to defend a citadel until relief came, but the besiegers were, in the meantime, discouraged by these methods of thinning their numbers.

In the completed Kenilworth the idea of active defence was further carried out. A curtain wall was built around the original buildings of the Inner Ward, making the castle roughly concentric in plan. Then it was necessary merely to connect the principal watercourses by ditches and to dam the main Finham Brook, in order to isolate the castle behind the almost impregnable defence of a lake half a mile in length, with a smaller lake on the eastern side of the dam. The parts of the curtain undefended by the lake were covered by broad moats.

These works narrowed the besiegers' point of attack. The dam became a causeway leading to the principal entrance. On the landward end was an earthwork called the Brayes, with its own gatehouse and with mounds on which to place engines of war. Behind this was a moat, and a drawbridge giving access to the Gallery Tower, which held the head of the dam, while at the far end of the narrow causeway was the strong Mortimer's Tower projecting from the curtain wall, a barbican in itself, forming a third line of defence. All these additions were probably made about the time of Henry III, so that they are contemporary in time and analogous in character to Caerphilly. Thus Kenilworth

KENILWORTH

is an illustration of the many valuable military lessons brought home from the East by the Crusaders.

It might be expected of a Midland castle, which defended England against no foreign enemy, that its history would be one of baronial ambition and of civil war. The nationalism of this country was hammered out on her borders and in France; but it cannot be said that the Barons' Wars and the Stuart Civil Wars did nothing for the development of her internal order.

The lordship of Kenilworth was granted by Henry I to his chamberlain, Geoffrey de Clinton, who, with his descendants, erected the castle. But the family soon died out. In the reign of Henry II the fortress had reverted to the King, who defended it against his rebellious sons, and it may be that the stone keep was erected by the monarchy. Certainly, John saw the value of the place. He expended the large sum of £937 upon its restoration and improvement, and naturally refused to surrender it to the Barons to whom he had promised it at Runnymede. Henry III also strengthened the castle, and in 1253 he granted it, foolishly enough, to his son-in-law, Simon de Montfort, Earl of Leicester, under whose followers it endured its memorable siege.

Kenilworth was one of the main centres of the baronial strength in the Midlands. Under its walls Prince Edward stole upon the forces of the younger Simon when they were resting after a tiring march; and Simon alone, clad in a shirt, managed to escape in a boat across the lake to the castle. A few days later came the news of the battle of Evesham, and Kenilworth was converted from a hotbed of revolt to a last refuge of the rebels. Nevertheless, it sustained a six months' siege. Henry III brought up towers and siege engines to the north curtain, but could make no impression. He ordered barges overland from Chester and attempted an attack from the lake, but with no success, for the audacious rebels even kept the gates open day and night, making frequent and damaging sorties. When towers and barges had failed, the Papal legate, Cardinal Ottoboni, afterwards Pope Adrian V, was called upon to excommunicate the defenders, which he did; but they dressed one of their number in mockery of the legate, and from the battlements parodied the anathemas. In the end, although Simon himself submitted, the rest of the Disinherited, as they were called, held out until famine and dysentery compelled them to yield.

After its recovery to the Crown, Henry III granted Kenilworth to his son, Edmund Crouchback, Earl of Lancaster, through whom it descended ultimately to John of Gaunt. It is to the latter, a noble patron of architects, that Kenilworth owes the finer parts of its palace buildings, especially the hall, which may once have been the finest in England, even more beautiful than the well-preserved Westminster Hall, to judge from the oriel window, the panelled fireplaces, the high springing arches that remain.

But now we see only the hand of man, the destroyer, and of Time. Dudley " modernized " the keep and other portions after the Tudor manner, and the buildings that he erected were not fit to endure. The castle again suffered in civil war, and after being garrisoned by the Stuart Royalists it fell into the hands of the Parliamentarians, who deliberately ruined it. We have to thank one, Colonel Hawkesworth, and his Roundhead companions for the breached curtain walls, the towers blown up with gunpowder, and the keep laid open to the weather by the destruction of one wall. It was Hawkesworth, also, who drained the lake in order to cultivate the land around the castle. The water which had for so long mirrored the walls and towers ebbed away when the beautiful reality was shattered. And because the lake has disappeared, a modern visitor finds it nearly impossible to imagine either the strength or the majesty of the older Kenilworth. Let him try to visualize a tournament in progress in the Tilt Yard (half-way across the dam), with the towers behind and the water on either side. Or let him imagine Elizabeth's brilliant cavalcade riding up the causeway to Mortimer's Tower, being received by a person representing " one of the ten sibills, cumly clad in a pall of white silk, who pronounced a proper poesie in English rime and meeter." Then he will realize what Kenilworth has lost by the draining of its lake, and what England has lost in the dismantling of Kenilworth.

The military history of Kenilworth ended appropriately with a civil war, and of its vast range of buildings, to-day only the very pacific gatehouse built by Dudley in the north-east enclosure is fit for habitation; while its neighbour Warwick has survived gloriously as a palace-castle.

KENILWORTH CASTLE.

RICHMOND AND BARNARD

THERE are curious analogies to be found between Richmond and Barnard, which resemble each other in situation, in origin, and in their historical connection. The two castles are little more than sixteen miles apart, and it is possible to imagine an all-embracing local patriotism impartially proud of both. But there is a world of difference between Swaledale and Teesdale, between Yorkshire and Durham. Yorkshiremen point out that Barnard possesses the beauty but lacks the strength of Richmond, and only a few miles away public opinion declares that Richmond is indeed beautiful but lacking the dominance of Barnard. Swinburne compared Richmond with Toledo, and one writer, indulging in what is surely a mixed metaphor, referred to the Yorkshire Heidelberg. Sir Walter Scott, on the other hand, devoted his praise in *Rokeby* to " proud Barnard's bannered walls," and " Brackenbury's dungeon tower."

At least the two castles are alike, and who is to measure the perfection of their attributes ? A first impression of Richmond is of a swift river, a graceful bridge, and behind these the rising hill topped by walls and towers and the great dominating keep. It is built upon a spur projecting from the side of the valley towards the Swale, and in conformity with its site the castle is roughly triangular in plan, the longest side of the enclosure resting upon the summit of the cliffs above the river on the south, and the apex, defended by the keep, overlooking the town of Richmond on the north. The platform upon which the castle stands is 150 feet above the Swale, and from the battlements of the keep (which is 100 feet in height) may be seen the three towers of York Minster, forty miles away.

No attack could ever be made with any hope of success from the direction of the river. The bush-clad slopes of the hill become sharply graduated ledges out of which spring the buttresses and walls of the curtain, which is still tolerably perfect. On the northern side, towards the town, a narrower front was protected by a dry ditch, which has since been covered over and built upon. The keep was at the salient point of the defences. It projected from the curtain wall, covered by a barbican (now in ruins), and it commanded the entrance to the triangular main ward. The walls of Richmond were built in stone immediately after the Conquest, probably in 1071, and the keep was not added until the time of Henry II. By a happy inspiration the builders placed it, not in the corner of the enclosure farthest from the entrance, but at a point where it had to serve as a first line of defence. This doubled the strength of the castle, for the large main ward was obviously built to accommodate not only the garrison but also the people of the surrounding country, who might come there for a refuge with their flocks; and although the strength of a place formed by a keep and with an adjacent enclosure as a rule lay chiefly in the keep, at Richmond the disposition of parts and the nature of the site produced a balanced system of mutual defence. The risk of starvation was also reduced: the enclosure became a capacious and well-protected granary.

At the eastern side of the enceinte, where the ground sloped only gradually, was a smaller flanking ward, called the Cockpit. In addition to these natural and artificial protections were the walls of the town, ordered to be built by Edward II against the irruptions of the Scots. Leland wrote: " Richemonte towne is waulled and the Castel on the river side of Swale is as the knot of the cumpace of the waul." But in his day the castle was " a mere ruine," and of the town walls only " vestigia " remained.

From the inner side it is easily seen that the keep was built actually upon the wall of the enceinte. The stone courses of the wall form the south side of the basement and a Norman arch gives access to it. This must once have been defended by a forebuilding, and before the keep was added it was probably the main entrance to the enclosure. But Richmond keep is none the less strong for that improvisation. It may be coupled with Porchester as having been built for purely military purposes, with thick walls leaving little inside space, narrow loops for windows, and no real provision for domestic life.

No doubt an unusually complete series of domestic buildings was in existence at Richmond before the keep was begun. It is usually accepted (though not entirely without bickerings among the learned) that Scolland's Hall and the group of buildings in the south-east corner of the enclosure date back to the third quarter of the eleventh century. Scolland's Hall, which is well preserved, stands against the south curtain. It is in two floors, and the basement was probably intended as a storeroom and looped for defence. The hall proper was entered by an exterior stair through a round-headed archway flanked by Norman pillars. Light was given by ranges of coupled round-headed windows at the sides and by a triplet of narrow windows at the west end. The Scollands were the lords of Bedale, powerful feudatories of the Honour of Richmond. There are those who ascribe the building to John of Gaunt, and the name to the fact that it was built on the site of what had been known as Scolland's Tower from an earlier period. In fact, there does seem to be a reason why the Scollands should give their name to a tower and no other obvious reason why they should give it to the hall of the castle, but if the hall can be said to be Norman it is one of the best and earliest examples in the country. One day the awkward problem will be solved, but at present it is merely an indication of how difficult it is to date a building by stonework alone without documentary evidence. But in Robin Hood's Tower the arcaded Norman chapel dedicated to St. Nicholas was the first chapel of the castle, and there is documentary evidence to show that it was granted as a cell to the Abbey of St. Mary, in York, during the lifetime of the Conqueror. This little oratory measures 10 feet by 12 feet, yet it has aisles or mural arcades of five arches each.

Richmond Castle is of immense strength, and its warlike aspect has so impressed itself upon the minds of men that it seems to be part of the web and woof of English history. It is difficult to imagine the story of Richmond set down without a catalogue of valiant knights, crossbowmen, divers great bombards, and the " pulvis ad faciendum le krak," as a chronicler called gunpowder. At least one would imagine it as a base in the Scottish wars, besieged in the Wars of the Roses, or held by Royalist against Roundhead. But, in point of fact, Richmond has never been taken by storm or even assaulted. The march and counter march of wars left it on one side. It served as a prison for William the Lion, David Bruce, and Charles I, in their various captivities. It gave the title of Earl to " Harry of Richmond," later Henry VII, and he bestowed the name upon another mound by the Thames (now a suburb of wide-flung London), where stood the royal palace of Sheen. A Duke of Richmond was Henry Fitzroy, the natural son of Henry VIII; and Charles II granted the title of Duke of Richmond to Charles Lennox, son of Louise de Kerouaille. But the first lords of Richmond made a deeper impression upon the place than any of their successors.

Before the Conquest the hill of Richmond, probably unfortified, was in the district of Gillingshire, held by Edwin, last Earl of Mercia. But with the Conqueror came Alan the Red, nephew of the Duke of Brittany, with a host of brothers determined to make their fortunes. Ribald, the youngest, became Lord of Middleham, Brian became Earl of Cornwall, Alan the Red became Earl of Richmond, and dying without issue was succeeded in the title by two more brothers, Alan the Black and Stephen. Alan received Edwin's Gillingshire and other lordships —a total of 440 manors, indicative of the assistance rendered to William by the well-trained Bretons. His power was such that he was often called the " Prince of the East Angles," and he brought many of his own race to Yorkshire. There is an old Yorkshire rhyme about the Breton who

> Came out of Brittany
> With his wife Tiffany
> And his maid Manfras
> And his dog Hardigras.

Many of the local names at Richmond are equally foreign to Yorkshire. There is a particular interest, then, in the legend that underneath Richmond keep King Arthur and his knights are slumbering, awaiting the hour of England's greatest need. Before them, on a stone table, lie Excalibur and a battle trumpet, until a brave man comes who will draw the one or blow the other. It is a legend that relates to many places in Celtic lands, but not in England. The Bretons themselves speak of the Island of Agalon, off Brittany, as Arthur's sleeping place.

The Breton earls, in the ambiguous position of great landowners and feudatories on both sides of the Channel, between the millstones of England and France though they were, survived in some fashion at Richmond until John of Gaunt was created Earl by Edward III. Conan, who built or began the building of the keep, was the most glorious of them all. He combined the Duchy of Brittany with the Earldom of Richmond, and married the sister of William the Lion. Their daughter was Shakespeare's Constance, wife of Geoffrey Plantagenet, son of Henry II, and mother of that Prince Arthur of Brittany who suffered as one of the victims of King John. After that we find the Yorkshire castle in precarious tenure, for on an occasion of war with France, the English king seized the Earldom of Richmond on the plea that it was a foreign fief, and the French king seized the Dukedom of Brittany for the same reason, leaving the unfortunate possessor of both titles in no little uncertainty as to his future and allegiance.

Barnard Castle, now in a more ruinous condition than Richmond, was named after its founder, Bernard Balliol, the son of Guy of Bailleul, another companion of the Conqueror. No doubt the castle took final form at the end of the twelfth century, but it shows the marks of subsequent alteration and embellishments. It was used as a dwelling-place longer than Richmond, and shows far more the characteristics of a palace, such as it would acquire in the fourteenth and fifteenth centuries. The keep, called Balliol's Tower, is in reality a circular tower of the fourteenth century, and it is noticeable that the old curtain walls near it have been pierced with decorated windows and strengthened with buttresses, in the combined interests of peace and war. Bernard's castle was no doubt only the inner ward, surrounded by a ditch 70 feet wide, but to this was soon added the outer, middle, and town wards, all of which could be defended separately.

The connection of Richmond with Brittany has its parallel in the connection of Barnard with Scotland, for the Balliols were, of course, claimant to the Scottish throne, but after John Balliol's defeat at Dunbar, in 1296, it came into the hands of the Bishop of Durham. Later, Barnard was held by Guy Beauchamp, Earl of Warwick, and by Richard, Duke of Gloucester, afterwards Richard III. The latter's cognizance, the bristly boar, may be

seen sculptured upon the projecting oriel window west of Balliol's Tower.

Despite its strength, Richmond was already neglected and decayed at the beginning of the fifteenth century, but Barnard, which is now the more dilapidated of the two, stood siege in the Rising of the North, when Sir George Bowes held it for the Queen until his garrison deserted him. That was Barnard's last experience of warfare, but it survived in tolerable repair up to 1630, when the castle was sold, dismantled, and many of its fittings carried away for the embellishment of Raby, which is to-day an inhabited castle, one of the most perfect in the north of England.

BARNARD CASTLE.

THE TOWER OF LONDON

SHAKESPEARE paid homage to a common opinion, resting on " none assured ground " (as Stowe declared), when he described the Tower of London as " Julius Cæsar's ill-erected tower." On its site there was indeed the *Arx Palatina*, a Roman stronghold, remains of which have been unearthed in recent years within the precincts of the Tower; but Stowe correctly pointed out in his " Survey of London," that " the original author and founder as well of this as also of many other towers, castels, and great buildings within the Realm " was William the Conqueror, who not later than 1078 saw the massive walls of the White Tower rise up under the direction of Gundulph, Bishop of Rochester, known to his contemporaries as " the weeping monk of Bec."

Possibly Gundulph was plunged into gloom by the realization that his Benedictine habit concealed a genius in the science of military architecture, but his sorrow did not interfere with his work. This, the earliest and most famous of the Norman keeps in England, was intended to outlast history itself; as indeed it seemed to do when Londoners began to call it Cæsar's. The stones were selected, and of proved strength; the walls varied from 10 feet to 15 feet in thickness, the mortar binding the stones of the lower courses, far from being " tempered with the bloud of beasts," as a later tradition held, was a more practical compound of lime and cockle shells; while the keep was divided, to increase its strength, by an internal cross-wall from basement to battlement, between 10 feet and 6 feet in width. There was no military engine of the day that could damage the White Tower, and, as the science of warfare improved, monarch after monarch threw around it moat and wall, and a girdle of strong towers.

By the time of Edward III's death, the fortress stood complete. It faced the river on ground gently rising to Tower Hill. The keep was surrounded by a wall studded with twelve round towers, which are famous by their various names—the Bloody Tower, the Beauchamp, the Devereux, to recall a few—for their associations with prisoners of high rank, and even with murders done by royal command. These towers enclosed the Palace Ward, for between the keep and the south wall was the royal palace, swept away by Cromwell and the Stuarts to make room for storehouses. Around the defence of the Palace Ward, and very close to it, was the outer wall, making between a narrow ward, in which an enemy, were he able to enter it, would find himself without cover from missiles and without room to manœuvre a battering ram. This was only one of the difficulties of an attacking force, which would have had to cross a broad moat supplied from the Thames in order to make a breach in the outer defences. The moat was filled up by the Duke of Wellington when he held the position of Constable of the Tower, on account of its effects upon the health of the garrison; and no doubt in its day it killed as many people as the headsman's axe.

It was Henry III (a builder with an outstanding reputation, if it rested on nothing else than his work at Westminster and Windsor) who constructed "the wharf" as a protection: a broad walk like the Embankment, formed of rubble thrown down between piles. Spanning the moat to the wharf was St. Thomas' Tower, in reality a barbican, since the entrance from the river was by a wonderfully engineered gateway at its base, known to history as Traitors' Gate, through which have passed some of England's finest and some of her vilest men. The tower, which contains a

THE TOWER OF LONDON

little oratory dedicated to St. Thomas-à-Becket, must have been named after that saint as a peace offering.

Naturally enough Londoners had no love for the royal fortress, typifying as it did the power of the monarchy in the very face of their civic independence and, as Henry III had difficulties and disasters in the course of his building, the townsfolk ascribed them to the judgments of Heaven. Even more galling to a Plantagenet, they said it was a judgment of St. Thomas; and in a vision the murdered Archbishop was seen by " a holy and discreet priest," overturning the walls with his crozier. The visionary also reported that St. Thomas accompanied his devastating labours by the quaint remark that if he himself had not found the occasion to ruin the work, St. Edmund or some other saint most certainly would have done so. But Henry persevered, and to-day Londoners are proud of the walls that so much displeased their ancestors.

As a prison the Tower of London retains its romantic interest to the full, however little it is now a menace or a defence for London, even with its regimental garrison and its sturdy Beefeaters. But the chain of prisoners which began with Ralph Flambard (who soon enough let himself down the wall by a rope, firmly grasping his crozier) perhaps did not end with the brave spy, Lieutenant Lodi, or with Roger Casement. Between the two extremes of type and time, between the Bishop and the spy, is a succession that has left a long tale of intrigue, of torture, of death, sometimes of escape, and a group of inscriptions cut or painted upon the prison walls, which forms a sort of marginal annotation to the history of the country. Most pathetic of all is the inscription " IANE," in the Beauchamp Tower, traditionally the work of Guildford Dudley, whose wife, Lady Jane Grey, was also imprisoned nearby. The Dudleys, the Fitzgeralds of Kildare, and the Poles (who were of royal blood, and therefore dangerous to the Tudors) were among the families which were practically extirpated by imprisonment in the Tower. Arthur Pole left a beautiful inscription: " I. H. S. A passage perillus maketh a porte pleasant. Ao. 1568." There is a grim complaint in the Beauchamp Tower: " By tortyre straynge mi troyth was tryed yet of my liberty denied 1581 Thomas Myagh."

Of those who were condemned to death a favoured few were executed at the block within the fortress on Tower Green. These were Anne Boleyn, Katherine Howard, the Countess of Salisbury, Viscountess Rochford, Lady Jane Grey, and Devereux, Earl of Essex. The last-named owed the comparative privacy of his death to the fickle favour of Elizabeth, and the others to their sex, for there is no record of any woman being executed in public on Tower Hill, where so many Englishmen died; some, like Sir Thomas More, with a smile, and some like the Duke of Monmouth, in agony, for the axe, in his case, was blunt, and the executioner nervous.

Unless the body of the sufferer was granted to relatives, it was brought back for burial to the Church of St. Peter-ad-Vincula, in the Palace Ward, founded by Henry I and rebuilt by Henry VIII, who had need of it for his many victims. Queen Anne Boleyn and Queen Katherine Howard lie together in death; Cardinal Fisher and Sir Thomas More were brought here for burial a short time before Thomas Cromwell, who gave evidence against them; and here the Jacobite lords, Balmerino, Kilmarnock and Lovat were given at least a better grave than the seventy-odd Scotch prisoners of the '45, who were imprisoned in a dungeon in the Wakefield Tower, where many of them died for want of air and food.

There are good stories to tell of escapes from the Tower. Not the least daring was that of Father Gerard, the Jesuit, who let himself down by a rope to a boat in the Thames, despite the fact that he had been suspended in iron clamps by his hands for such long periods that they were paralysed; or that of the Jacobite Lord Nithsdale who, by the devotion of his wife, escaped disguised as a serving maid on the eve of his execution.

As for the other associations of the Tower, who has not heard of the cell named " Little Ease," of the young Princes buried hugger-mugger at the foot of the chapel stairs that they might lie in some sort within consecrated ground; and who wishes to hear again of the " Scavenger's daughter," the thumbscrews, or the racks which the Tudors used so constantly, under the direction of wretches like Wriothesley and Topcliffe?

But, although the human interest of the Tower can never be exhausted, one cannot ignore the institutions or the buildings that grew up within its walls. Architecturally the Chapel of St. John the Evangelist is one of the finest pieces of Norman work now preserved to us. It is on the second floor of the White Tower, its crypt below, and above, forming a triforium arcade, is the mural gallery which runs around the whole wall of the third floor, so that it is evident how far the Norman builders considered a chapel one of the structural necessities of a keep. Subsequently, however, it fell upon evil days. Robbed of statues and stained glass, it was filled with a confused mass of putrefying documents, which were actually a danger on account of " the cankerous smell and evil scent "; but it was cleared in the last century, fortunately before the army clothing department was able to carry out a design to convert it into a tailor's warehouse.

In the White Tower also was the Council Chamber, and the room where the judge of the King's Bench sat long ago, while the Court of Common Pleas was held in the hall of the palace, now swept away. The Mint, once one of many, was established in the fortress which was always the natural stronghold for the king's treasure, and is still the depository for the regalia.

THE TOWER OF LONDON

It is evident, then, that in the late war the Germans showed some insight into the meaning of history when they made a special attack upon the Tower of London. An unexploded bomb or two were found in the ground, a small window was broken in the Wakefield Tower, and a pigeon was killed, while German cartoonists and medallists were delighting their compatriots with pictures of London Bridge fallen down at last, and the Tower a burning ruin; for what we call morale is a pride in past traditions, and the spirit of England would have suffered in the destruction of the Tower.

THE TOWER OF LONDON (THE MIDDLE GATEWAY).

WARWICK

QUITE apart from its history, Warwick Castle itself satisfies our ideas about the surroundings of mediæval chivalry, partly because it is so well maintained by the present Earls, and partly on account of its architectural features. It is a castle of bold effects and sweeping lines, in many ways more French than English in its inspiration. The massive strength of the barbican and gatehouse is relieved by the tall towers behind, connected high in the air by a graceful stone arch; Guy's Tower and Cæsar's Tower, both polygonal, stand like tall sentinels at the flanks of the northern curtain wall; and, on the southern side, the broad sweep of the palace itself extends along the bank of the Avon, which flows below past the ruins of the old bridge. Certainly, if Warwick could still boast the shell keep upon the mound at the western end of the enceinte, it would be known as one of the most splendid of European castles.

Warwick, in common with most of the English castles, has been ascribed to the Romans. The later twelfth-century circular keep at Conisborough was, according to a triumphant antiquary, " built and in use in Pagan times," and he even found within it " a niche for an idol "; and Restormel was " even of earlier date than Conisborough itself." From the same source we learn that the Norman keep at Norwich is " a most noble specimen of Saxon architecture," for " certain it is that all its ornaments are in the true Saxon style," while Colchester was the work of Edward the Elder.

So, in consideration especially of the ground plan of Warwick, one is doubtful also of its ascription to Ethelfleda, " the lady of the Mercians," as a part of the reconquest of the Danelaw carried out under Alfred's successors. Possibly the mound was thrown up by the Saxons, though more likely the Saxon defensive work took the form of a stockade around the town of Warwick. The actual castle, as we see it—in the Norman form of a mound surmounted by a keep with a walled enclosure adjacent to it—was undoubtedly founded by William the Conqueror on his way north after the siege of Exeter. But the connection between Ethelfleda and William lies in the fact that Warwick is one of an almost complete series of castles on or near the county towns. The shire system, which spread through England with the expansion of Wessex, was taken over for military, judicial, and fiscal purposes by the adaptable Normans.

The ground plan of Warwick is, in fact, surprisingly Norman. The earliest of its buildings, as they stand to-day, probably does not go back before the end of the thirteenth century, and one might expect a score of modifications in the ground plan to have been introduced by the active Earls of Warwick, who would be in a position to profit by the experiences of the Crusades and foreign wars. Perhaps the absence of the keep (the ruins of which were noted, however, by Leland, the Tudor antiquarian) is a case in point. It may have been gutted in Tudor times; but, on the other hand, it may have gradually fallen into disrepair when the strength of the curtain walls began to be of more importance than the strength of the citadel. For the rest, the situation of the domestic buildings along the east wall of the enclosure is in keeping with the dispositions of a Norman mound-and-bailey castle.

In the elaboration of the barbican and the projection of the corner towers the ground plan betrays work of post-Norman builders which is unmistakable in elevation. The military aspect of Warwick continued to be emphasized during a period in which other English castles were becoming palaces and manor

WARWICK

houses, and the manifestation of a French tradition at Warwick reflects the fact that the science of castellation was being forgotten in this country. The founder of the present building is believed to have been Thomas Beauchamp, Earl of Warwick, who led the English vanguard at Poitiers. He died in 1369 of a disease contracted during the campaign, and the work carried on by his son was completed in 1394.

The most commanding features are the two polygonal towers on the flanks of the northern curtain wall. In every characteristic they approximate to the French tradition inaugurated by Philip Augustus. Guy's Tower, 128 feet high, may be contrasted with that of the contemporary rectangular towers at Raby, the loftiest of which is only 81 feet high, and depends for its strength upon the thickness of its walls. Guy's Tower and Cæsar's Tower have more strategic value. Their parapets are boldly corbelled outwards with a row of machicolations, and they are provided with central turrets rising some distance above the level of the rampart walk. The floors of both towers are strongly vaulted as though to enable them to bear the weight of siege engines. It is interesting, by the way, to notice that castle towers sank with the increased use of artillery. The weight of the gun, the shock of its recoil, the low trajectory of its fire, led to the introduction of the low drum tower, which finally sank to the bastion perfected by Vauban in France, so that the high towers of Warwick mark the perfection of a mediæval tradition that was soon to die out.

The barbican and gatehouse in the same curtain wall complete an inspiring picture. The barbican is flanked by drum towers pierced with cruciform loops. On the heavy iron hooks which stud the towers, wool sacks are said to have been hung as a defence against musketry in Warwick's last defence against the Roundheads. The archway of the barbican contains a portcullis, still in working order, and heavy double doors. The barbican passage, resembling that of Alnwick, is long and narrow, with galleries in its walls, so that an almost inviolable protection is given to the gatehouse, above and behind which is the building called the Clock Tower, joined by an upper story and by a stone bridge at the level of the ramparts.

Of the other towers, the Bear and Clarence Towers on the west side are either ruined or unfinished. But the history of Warwick's purely military fortifications does not end with the Middle Ages, for the gatehouse on the western curtain and the Water Gate between the mound and the domestic buildings are both of the seventeenth century, and both have stood a siege.

The older Warwick was a pivotal point in the Evesham campaign, and in 1321 the Earls of Hereford and Lancaster held it against the monarchy. But the present structure is bound up with the families of Beauchamp, Earls of Warwick, the Nevilles, and the Grevilles, who now hold the title. The story of the King Maker besieged in such a castle as this would make interesting reading, but, unfortunately, the Wars of the Roses were a series of campaigns in open country with few sieges.

James I granted Warwick to Sir Fulke Greville, the ancestor of the present owner, who spent large sums in restoration, and only just in time. For, in the Civil Wars, Warwick was on the Parliamentary side and besieged by Lords Northampton and Derby. In this case, as in many others during the Civil Wars, the splendid promise given by artillery at Bamburgh was belied. No immediate breach was made in the strong walls, and although Sir Edward Peto, captain of the garrison, hoisted a winding sheet and a Bible expressing both his expectations and his trust, the garrison was successfully relieved by Greville, who was himself shortly afterwards killed at Lichfield.

The domestic buildings are largely of the late fourteenth

century. The internal decorations were carried out in Stuart days, except for those parts which were gutted by fire one hundred years ago. The hall lost in the fire its old furnishings, but the Grevilles were assisted by the whole nation to rebuild the historic residence. In the course of this restoration the roof was raised, the old clerestory windows restored, and the polished floor of red and white marble was brought from Venice. Fortunately the priceless collection of paintings, the fruit of many a Grand Tour in the eighteenth century, was preserved from the flames, and only a portion of the collection of armour was destroyed.

Warwick Castle, then, is simple in plan, but ideally picturesque. It has grace combined with its strength. It is an ornament to a beautiful county, and a curious example of an English castle in which the military and domestic aspects are held in a just and natural balance.

THE CASTLES OF NORTH WALES

IT seems a far cry from Carnarvon to Constantinople, from the castle of Krak des Chevaliers, in the County of Tripoli, to Harlech, on the cliffs of Wales. Yet it is to the Orient that one must go for the inspiration of the concentric type of fortress, which is seen at its best in the castles built by Edward I to subdue the Welsh. For Constantinople faithfully preserved the traditions of the Roman Empire. The Crusaders brought back to Europe from the East much that the West had forgotten during five centuries; and as the Byzantine Empire was not a dead limb of corruption (*pace* Gibbon), they brought back these military ideas improved and refined by a people which had fought continually to reconquer its lost territories. The Crusaders were astonished to find at Constantinople a triple wall three miles in extent with a hundred flanking towers; and the outer walls were lower than the inner so that the soldiers of the triple line of defence could shoot simultaneously at the enemy. The walls at Constantinople were of the same lineage as those at Pevensey, but of a later generation. To imitate the simile contained in a well-known poem, it might be said that the builders of Carnarvon went to Pevensey by way of the Golden Horn.

At the sieges of Acre and Antioch the Crusaders found that they had to capture the flanking towers—veritable fortresses in themselves—before they could carry the walls commanded by them. The Franks in Syria built many notable fortifications in which advantage was taken of their experience in the new tactical plan. Even the ruins of such strongholds as Kerak in the desert beyond Jordan, and Krak des Chevaliers, rival in dignity the walls of Carnarvon and Conway.

The new ideas spread very gradually through Europe, from the time when Richard I, acting on first-hand knowledge, erected his Château Gaillard, which was, however, built to oppose successive lines of defence to the enemy rather than as a network of fortifications in which each section assisted another. The ideal castle would be capable of defence by the smallest possible garrison in proportion to the size of the army of attack; it would allow a party from the garrison to make a sortie from one point in order to attack an enemy force that was engaged elsewhere in an assault; it would therefore oblige the besieger to weaken his forces by dividing them so as to cover all the defences, and it would be so situated by sea or river as to allow a relieving party to reach the castle without passing through the besieger's lines. In the ideal castle of the type, siege engines could not be brought up to walls enfiladed by flanking towers, and these towers with the gatehouses could hold out by themselves for a time as isolated citadels if every other part of the defences were captured by the attackers. The fruition of these ideas is still to be seen in the famous defences of Carcassonne in France, which were erected after the Albigensian Crusade at a time contemporary with the building of Caerphilly.

The Welsh castles were not, like most of the English castles, adapted for successive military needs. It is possible to trace the evolutionary growth of the Tower of London, of Dover, and even of the border-line castles at Chepstow and Ludlow. Because few castles were built on new sites in England after the reign of Henry II, the English castles were for the most part makeshift in the best sense of the word. Lessons learnt abroad and at home had to be applied to existing castles. Ingenious barbicans and flanking towers were added to the Norman walls, and a compromise had to be hammered out between the military and the domestic aspects; but the English castles were none the less strong for that, and the early splendour of their domestic buildings reflects the rise of a capable monarchy.

But it was otherwise in Wales. There, until the middle of the fourteenth century, castles were built for immediate military purposes. The chains of castles extending to Pembroke and northward up the river valleys; from Shrewsbury into the mountains; and from Chester to Criccieth, were block-houses to hold each new conquest. They were built rapidly in most cases, but always to a design carefully suited to the nature of the site. The military element was predominant; there was little room for the more refined comforts of English baronial life. And the royal castles, in North Wales in particular, proved almost by their existence that they were no longer needed. That the King could build Conway or Beaumaris was an indication that he had conquered, that there was the less need for such castles. Possibly Wales might still have been lost without them, but by the time of the Wars of the Roses they stood for no more and no less than any of the royal castles in England. They stood for the struggle between Lancastrian and Yorkist, not for the English against the Welsh. And because they were built at a late period with scientific care, they remain without alterations and improvements at the hands of later generations as examples of the highest level to which the art of castellation rose in these islands during the Middle Ages.

There is a strange story that in the reign of Henry I a Syrian named Lalys was settled in Glamorgan by Richard de Glanville. He lived at Lalestown, assisted in the first buildings at Neath Abbey, and presumably left his mark upon the castles in the neighbourhood; but he made no impression upon the general history of military architecture. In 1277 when Edward I, upon the submission of Llewelyn, immediately began the erection of Rhuddlan, he employed as his architect a man with the high-sounding name of Master James de St. George, whom we find engaged at a later period on Conway, Harlech, and Beaumaris. It has been suggested that the architect of Harlech must have been responsible also for Caerphilly, but little is certainly known of Master James de St. George, except that he was the *magister operacionum regis in Wallia*, drawing at one period a salary of three shillings a day in the money of the time, and later a yearly retaining fee of one hundred marks.

The many strongholds which this architect may have planned were intended to blockade Snowdonia. Some of these were Welsh fortresses originally, reconstructed by the victorious English. It is curious that the Welsh ever took to castle-building. The mountains were sufficient defences in themselves when the plains had been surrendered. Edward's military problem might be compared with the siege of a Norman castle. Snowdonia was an impregnable keep with Anglesey and the coastal strip an enclosure or granary at its foot. If the Welsh were to build castles anywhere they should have built them in the flat lands. But such castles as Criccieth, Harlech, Bere, and Dolwyddelan, in various states of disrepair, are the eagles' nests of the defeated Welsh, occupied by the victors; while in the lowlands we find Conway, Carnarvon, Beaumaris, and Rhuddlan among those built on new sites by the English invaders.

Harlech stands boldly upon a rock 200 feet in height, with a sandy plain at its foot separating it from the sea. It belongs to the orthodox concentric type, for its lines of defence lie one within another; but it is not built on a geometric plan like Beaumaris, for the walls follow the contour of the rock, and are built to command a frontage on the sea whence relief could arrive during a siege. The outer ward, irregular in shape, made

a large enclosure to the north of the main fortifications, taking in the slopes of the hill down to the sea. On the west side was the water-gate, defended by a pit and a drawbridge. Thence a steep path, the way from the marsh, led upward, commanded at all points from the walls of the enclosure, to an upper gate in the wall, defended in the same manner. A survey taken in the reign of Henry VIII describes how this cleverly-protected " Weye from the Marshe," with a drawbridge at the lower level " to issew forthe horsemen or footemen, is forced upon the side of the rocke, having a strong wall towards the sea, being in length to another drawbridge c yerdes."

The square-set buildings of the castle itself stand at the south-east corner of this enclosure at the summit of the rock, surrounded at a slightly lower level by the walls of the middle ward with bastions at three of the angles and a barbican in front of the great gatehouse on the landward side. The walls of the outer enclosure joined the curtain of the middle ward in the southern and eastern sides, so at that point there were only two lines of defence. To remedy the defect a deep fosse was cut in the solid rock. The inner ward, roughly square, with round towers projecting at the angles, was very well protected from attack on three sides by the declivity of the hill, out of which the walls rose to a height of 40 feet.

At Harlech there was only one gatehouse, not two as at Beaumaris and elsewhere. This was a square building astride the wall projecting from the curtain towards the town in two rounded towers, its rear forming a rectangular block in the inner ward with round towers at the angles. The only feasible approach to the castle, then, was by ditch and barbican, and through the passage of the gatehouse, 54 feet in length, obstructed by three gates and three portcullises with a *meurtrière* opening at each end. Still the most perfectly preserved portion of Harlech castle, the gatehouse has three floors containing the private dwelling rooms of the Constable, with two private oratories, and guardrooms. Around the other walls of the ward were the quarters of the garrison, now largely destroyed; but they included a hall, kitchens, and a chapel.

The rebuilding of Harlech was probably begun in 1283, immediately after the death of Llewelyn and the capture of David, and there is probably no part of the castle later than the reigns of Edward I or his son. It maintained a garrison of no more than thirty men, which was yet large enough to defend the castle for three months in 1293. In the rising of Owen Glendower the castle was manned by only five Englishmen and fifteen Welshmen; but even after the capture of the Constable " the remnent of the sowdiers kept the Castel welynough " until it was shamefully delivered up " for a certain sum of gold." Harlech was the last castle surrendered to the Yorkists in the Wars of the Roses, and the last to hold out for Charles I in the Civil Wars. On the first occasion the Constable Dafydd ab Jevan ab Einion, called upon to surrender to Edward IV, proudly replied that " he had kept a castle so long in France as to make all the old women in Wales talk of him, and he would keep this castle so long as to make all the old women in France talk of him." In 1604 it was reported that Harlech was " as yet kept in somme better reparacioun than anye of his Majesty's Castles in North Wales," so that it was well prepared to give Major-General Mytton a stout resistance, though it was held by only forty-five men, and surrendered in 1647.

Neither Conway nor Carnarvon are orthodox, concentric castles, inasmuch as in each case the two wards are adjacent on a narrow site, but all the other principles of the concentric type are implied in their construction. Conway closed the approach to Snowdonia by land and river. It replaced the Norman fortress of

Deganwy higher up the River Conway on the English side, and being on the Welsh bank it acted as a bridgehead for the safe-guarding of Edward's lines. Carnarvon, which was the Roman Segontium, held the end of the road at the mouth of the River Seiont. Although they resemble each other superficially in plan, it is not thought that the same architect was responsible for the two castles. The round towers of Conway with turrets only in the inner ward can never be confused with the gaunt, octagonal towers of banded limestone at Carnarvon, with high turrets rising above them. The Eagle tower at Carnarvon is capped by three turrets, which have been fancifully compared with the three feathers of the Principality; for tradition, if not history, points to the Eagle tower as the birthplace of the first Prince of Wales. Both at Conway and Carnarvon the walls of the tower meet in the castle walls. At Conway the north-western angle of the castle was inside the town, and at Carnarvon the length of the castle took the place of a town wall on the south. Thus the town was an outer bailey to the castle, but the possibility of the defection of the citizen was not unprovided for: this is evident from the concentration of arrow slits on the head of the street leading to Carnarvon castle, and on the ground before the main gate. The towers flanking the gate were thickly set with slits commanding every inch of the entrance—some of them pointing inwards to cover the Welsh in the rear as they battered against successive portcullises.

Conway castle, roughly oblong in plan, was divided into two wards by a thick wall near the middle of its longer sides. At either end were platforms defended by walls and bastions. There was no gatehouse. The approach from the town, led through an outer gate up a steep ascent, over a drawbridge thrown across the ditch separating town from castle, and then through an inner gate to the western platform. A sharp turn to the left led to the well-defended gateway of the outer ward. By this device of a right-angle turn an enemy could be taken in flank as he approached the gateway. A similar arrangement was in use at Beaumaris. The eastern platform gave access to the water-gate by the sea. A hall and chapel were ranged against the south side of the outer ward, but the hall was a poor one, for it followed the curve of the wall. In the inner ward was a further series of living apartments, including the royal quarters, and in the Queen's tower a beautiful apsidal oratory in three bays with a lancet window in each.

At Carnarvon the shape is rather that of a figure eight, for the sides are drawn in a little where the cross-wall divided the enclosure into two wards. The division has now entirely disappeared, making it possible to see from end to end of the castle. Where Conway had no gatehouse Carnarvon had two. The King's Gate, facing the town, is now the only entrance, for the Queen's Gate on the east is 25 feet from the ground and could only have been approached by a steeply rising bridge across the moat. These two gatehouses with the Eagle tower at the west end (which was virtually the keep or strong tower of the castle) were the pivotal features of the castle. There was also a postern. Apart from these strategic provisions for defence there was a quay by the river-side for ships to discharge cargo, and the long line of wall fronting the river was pierced with three rows of loops served by two mural galleries and the rampart walk. Conway was more economically defended, for attack was inevitably concentrated upon the only exposed point, the gateway, which was so well protected; but at Carnarvon the defensive measures were more thoroughly worked out, and an enemy would have to scatter his forces very widely to safeguard himself from being taken in the flank by a sortie.

The history of Conway was very much the history of Carnarvon. In 1295, when the building of Carnarvon was half finished, a son of Llewelyn roused the people to rebellion when a large number were in the town for a fair. The castle was taken, the Constable hanged, and Edward hurried into Wales for the last time. He was forced to retreat upon Conway, after losing his baggage train, and there he was perilously besieged, for a high tide prevented the boats containing his supplies from crossing the river. He was able to put down the rising within a year, however, but the rebuilding of Carnarvon was necessary—he ordered the Justices of Chester to find 100 masons for the royal works at Carnarvon—and to safeguard Anglesey he built Beaumaris at the opposite end of the Menai Straits. During Owen Glendower's rebellion Conway fell into the rebels' hands for a few days, but Sir John Chandos with twenty men-at-arms and eighty archers, beat off the rebel leader's attacks at Carnarvon in 1402. In the Civil Wars Conway, defended by Archbishop Andrews of York and Sir John Owen, and Carnarvon, defended by Lord Byron, were both invested and forced to surrender by Major-General Mytton.

Harlech, on a crag by the sea, is at its best in a storm of wind or by a bright moon, but Conway or Carnarvon deserve the sunlight. Conway rivals York as an example of a mediæval walled town, and excels York in that the castle is so nearly intact. It commands the town on a promontory of a higher level, as Carnarvon castle overshadows its town by the height of its curtain walls. Carnarvon castle is, however, the better preserved of the two, for its walls are kept free from ivy, and it has more historical associations as the castle of the Prince of Wales. Dr. Johnson was not alone in the appreciation of Carnarvon, which he expressed during his visit in 1774. " I did not think there had been such buildings," exclaimed this lover of London ways, " it surpassed my ideas."

TINTAGEL

TINTAGEL CASTLE.

TINTAGEL

THIS is Tintagel, the castle which no man has ever seen. Many centuries ago there was on this spot a castle so built that one portion rested upon a splintered cliff standing up by the sea; and upon the causeway which connected the splinter with the mainland one good knight could defy the whole chivalry of England. It may be that you have stood between the sea and the cliffs to observe how the causeway became a gap, and the gap a chasm. You may have walked amidst the ruins of the castle. But it was not Tintagel.

> The Knight's bones are dust,
> And his good sword rust;
> His soul is with the saints, I trust.

Perhaps you thought of Igraine the mother of Arthur, hiding in Tintagel, to whom, by the magic of Merlin, came Uther Pendragon during the dark night in which her husband perished in the shock of battle. Or you thought of the great combat waged upon the strand between Sir Marhaus, Knight of Ireland, and Sir Tristram of Lyonesse. Or you heard the harp of Tristram in the ruined tower, and the voice of Iseult la Belle, the sad Queen of Cornwall, whose love for the knight of Lyonesse was once the theme of song and romance.

But if the broken walls upon the cliffs reminded you of Arthur, you did not see Tintagel. You may, however, have seen the castle drawn with skill in an illuminated book of the Middle Ages. You may have seen it while you read Layamon, or Wace, or Geoffrey of Monmouth. For Tintagel was always the castle of the mind's eye, the castle in the air.

TINTAGEL

Tintagel was the Utopia of chivalry. It did not raise proud battlements above the earth, but rather it hung marvellously from heaven. Upon its shimmering towers Galahad and Arthur walked. From its unshadowed gates came the cavalcades of perfect knighthood. Portcullis and moat and drawbridge were as nothing in the path of good men, but for a man who wore his spurs without honour they were impassable.

We know now that the ideal of perfect chivalry was incapable of realization. Men were barbaric, irreligious, greedy for lands and power, more apt to abduct the damsel in distress than to rescue her. But it is enough that the ideal ever existed, that Tintagel was ever seen, even in imagination. Perhaps there was some knight in those dark days—St. Louis the true Roi Soleil of France, shall we say?—who translated into action the whole knightly code. At least Arthur and Tintagel in romance, Louis and his good seneschal de Joinville in history, are enough to shame our complacency. With all our philanthropists, our district visitors, our earnest workers, we are not the first to conceive an ideal and clothe it in actions.

None of the great fortresses—Dover, Corfe, Nottingham, Pontefract, and the rest—were made of anything but common stone. They were inhabited by men of clay; and Time the despoiler, Man the destroyer, now and always beleaguer them. Visitors gape at their dungeons and drop pebbles into the echoing depths of their wells. Proud Dover was captured by a handful of townsfolk during the Civil Wars; Corfe is a struggling ruin, Nottingham and Pontefract are only names. But, if men die and stones decay, legends are cherished. It may be that the ideal Arthur will arise to rescue England in the hour of greatest need. It may be that Tintagel will be built up once more, not stone by stone, but ideally in the minds of men.

NEWCASTLE

POSSIBLY a romantic child can still invest the keep of Newcastle with all the glories of flying pennons, fair ladies, and knights-at-arms. But for those who have found that history is not a tale of the unceasing triumphs of idealists, there comes a weariness of Utopian chivalry. It may be that King Arthur was a " parfit gentil knight " indeed, but who King Arthur actually was no historian can say. And everybody knows that Henry II, who built the keep at Newcastle, was a King of some merit, of some talent, endowed like the rest of us with a fluctuating tide of virtues and vices.

The ruins of Tintagel give licence to the imagination to reconstruct their airy pinnacles, their cloud-capped towers, in the most magnificent way conceivable. The keep at Newcastle is preserved before our eyes in a severely practical manner. In its position it is as if caught and held fast in a fork of railways. It may once have stood siege, it may once have been the prison of kings. But in later days it has served as a county gaol and it is the meeting-place of a society of antiquaries. As though, indeed, solicitous that a border hold should come to such base uses, a paternal railway company has erected, at suitable positions in the vicinity, tasteful walls capped by picturesque but useless battlements. The great keep, bereft of curtain wall and drawbridge, has had restored to it by a generation in love with the past some little of its ancient glory. And, indeed, in this Newcastle is more fortunate than Canterbury, whose keep was converted into a coal-hole to assuage, in some measure, the archæological zeal of a gas company.

NEWCASTLE

But do not say there is no Romance in Newcastle keep. The lonely cliff of Tintagel is no more romantic than the industrial town that has grown up around the fortress of Robert Curthose and Henry II. When knights-errant saw the pennons and banners, they knew whose castle they approached. So do we, by a low-hung cloud of trailing smoke, recognize the industrial town.

There live the magnates of the new feudalism. Their castle is a factory, their crest a hoarding, their motto a slogan. Bound by ties of "economic self-interest," rather than by those of thegnhood or of sergeantry, an army of workers garrison their factories and accept their bounty; an army greater and more dependent—and bound not for a mere forty days of service, but until death—than ever gathered under the banner of a Neville or a Pole. In the new feudalism as in the old, it is the reliance of the weak upon the strong. The only change is that the military reliance has become an economic one.

Is not Romance here? How spiritless in comparison are the green fields of Tintagel, unused by man and useless to him. In Newcastle there is life and history in the making.

In the more immediate surroundings of Newcastle keep there lies another equally vital contrast. The older feudalism, being the formation of local associations, was in part, at least, the result of poor communications. The king's peace and the king's power had a tendency to be restricted to the great high roads. The keep was the local defence or the local terror; when besieged it held out as best it might until its garrison starved or its besiegers withdrew. Its main characteristic was immobile strength.

But it is the improvement in communication that has made possible the new feudalism. The local associations become increasingly national and controlled by the State; and in war it is not the combatant with the strongest defence, but the combatant with the most effective communications that is victorious. Verdun would not have sustained siege any longer than isolated Mauberge if it had not had the railways in its rear; and the industrial magnate knows that his factories are useless without his strategic railways to provision them with raw materials.

So the lodger in a slum and the worker in a factory need sigh no longer for green fields and ivy-mantled castle ruins in which to reincarnate all their fancied heroes of vanished centuries. Let them look up on high to the factory chimneys against the black pall of the firmament. Let them consider the railway lines, how they run here and there carrying the merchants and the merchandise that, to them, mean life and livelihood. Let them scorn the old feudalism of Tintagel and reverence the new feudalism of Newcastle. Is not this the whole of their life, and is not life Romance?

THE CASTLE, NEWCASTLE.

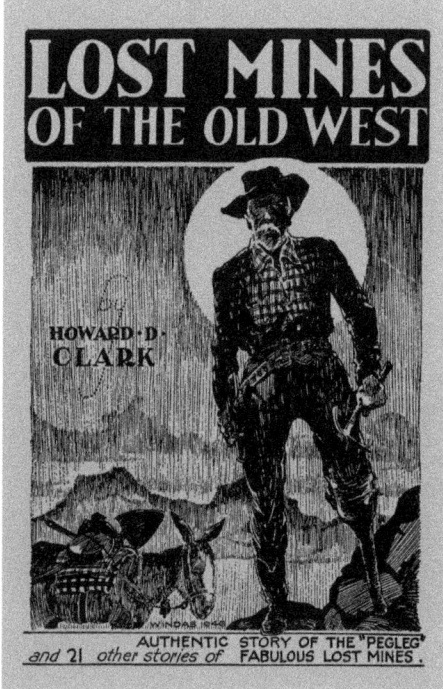

Coachwhip Publications
CoachwhipBooks.com

Coachwhip Publications
CoachwhipBooks.com

www.ingramcontent.com/pod-product-compliance
Lightning Source LLC
Chambersburg PA
CBHW060939170426
43195CB00022B/2977